TOUCH

The Centre for Attachment-based Psychoanalytic Psychotherapy

TOUCH

Attachment and the body

THE JOHN BOWLBY MEMORIAL CONFERENCE MONOGRAPH 2003

Edited by

Kate White

Published by
KARNAC BOOKS
for
THE CENTRE FOR ATTACHMENT-BASED
PSYCHOANALYTIC PSYCHOTHERAPY

Published in 2004 by
Karnac (Books) Ltd.
6 Pembroke Buildings, London NW10 6RE
on behalf of
The Centre for Attachment-based Psychoanalytic Psychotherapy

Opie, M. (2003). *Bowlby and Attachment*, Conference report in The Bridge, The Newsletter of the Association for Child Psychology and Psychiatry Issue 29, Spring 2003 page 5. Reprinted with permission of ACPP.

British Library Cataloguing in Publication Data

A C.I.P. for this book is available from the British Library

ISBN 1 85575 361 8

Edited, designed, and produced by The Studio Publishing Services Ltd, Exeter EX4 8JN

Printed in Great Britain

www.karnacbooks.com

CONTENTS

CONTRIBUTORS

Anne Aiyegbusi's professional position is Nurse Consultant—Women's Service—Broadmoor Hospital. Her role involves a therapy caseload, developing nursing practice, a role in strategic management of the women's directorate, providing supervision for nurses, teaching, and research. She is particularly interested in psychological trauma and the emotional impact on nursing staff of working with groups of traumatized women offenders. She has published several papers about women in secure care, the experience of black people in forensic mental health services, and self-injury. Anne has presented at conferences for many years.

Brett Kahr is Senior Lecturer in Psychotherapy in the School of Psychotherapy and Counselling at Regent's College in London; and in 2001, he became the inaugural Winnicott Clinic Senior Research Fellow in Psychotherapy. He has been a Consultant to the Centre for Attachment-Based Psychoanalytic Psychotherapy since its inception, as well as a longstanding member of its teaching and supervising staff. Additionally, he is a Patron of The Squiggle Foundation, and a Trustee of the Institute of Psychotherapy and Disability, as well as Special Media Adviser to The United Kingdom

Council for Psychotherapy. He works in private practice as a psychoanalytic psychotherapist and as a couple psychotherapist, having graduated from the Tavistock Marital Studies Institute. His books include *D. W. Winnicott: A Biographical Portrait*, which won the Gradiva Award for Biography in 1997; *Forensic Psychotherapy and Psychopathology: Winnicottian Perspectives*; and *The Legacy of Winnicott: Essays on Infant and Child Mental Health*, all published by Karnac, as well as a book on exhibitionism. He is the Series Editor of the Forensic Psychotherapy Monograph Series, also for Karnac.

Bernice Laschinger had many years of experience in community mental health before becoming an attachment-based psychoanalytic psychotherapist. She is a member of CAPP, where she is a training therapist, teacher, and supervisor, and has been very involved in the development of CAPP's training curriculum, particularly with the integration of the Relational model of pscyhoanalysis into the course.

Susie Orbach's interests as a psychotherapist and writer have centred around psychoanalysis, gender, counter-transference and the body, psychoanalysis and the public sphere, the construction of femininity and emotional literacy. Her first book, *Fat is a Feminist Issue*, is now twenty-three years old. It was followed by two books on eating problems, three on women's psychology with Luise Eichenbaum, and two collections of her Guardian columns called *What's Really Going on Here* and *Towards Emotional Literacy*. *The Impossibility of Sex*, imagined tales from therapy told from the psychotherapist's point of view, were published in 1999. In 1997 she co-founded The Women's Therapy Centre and in 1981 The Women's Therapy Centre Institute, a training institute in New York. She is currently Visiting Professor at the London School of Economics.

Margot Sunderland (UKCP Registered Psychotherapist) is Founding Director of the Centre for Child Mental Health, London. She is also Head of the Children and Young People Section of the United Kingdom Association for Therapeutic Counselling. Margot has several published books in child therapy, one of which won a BMA award (Mental Health section). Her main research area is "the neuroscience of human interaction". In addition, Margot is founding Director of "Helping Where It Hurts", which offers free therapy and counselling to troubled children in several primary schools in North London. The therapy work underwent Gulbenkian funded research showing successful outcomes. Margot is also Principal of The Institute for Arts in Therapy and Education, a fully accredited Higher Education college running a Diploma course in Child Therapy and Masters Degree courses in Art Psychotherapy and Arts in Education and Therapy.

Colwyn Trevarthen, a New Zealander, is Professor (Emeritus) of Child Psychology and Psychobiology of The University of Edinburgh, where he has taught since 1971. A biologist and psychologist, Trevarthen has published on neuropsychology, brain development and, in the last thirty years, on communication in infancy. He and colleagues have produced a book entitled *Children with Autism*, published by Jessica Kingsley and now in its second edition. Research on the infant mind began with Jerome Bruner at Harvard in 1966. The development of human "intersubjectivity", the ability to sympathize with other persons' mental states of all kinds, became his main line of work. He contributed the lead article to a book entitled *Intersubjective Communication and Emotion in Early Ontogeny*, edited by Stein Bråten and published by Cambridge University Press in 1998. Professor Trevarthen has an Honorary Doctorate in Psychology from the University of Crete, and he has been elected Fellow of the Royal Society of Edinburgh and Member of the Norwegian Academy of Sciences and Letters.

Kate White is a registered Member of the Centre for Attachment-based Psychoanalytic Psychotherapy where she has been Chair of the Education Committee, and is a training therapist, supervisor, and teacher. Formerly senior lecturer at South Bank University in the Department of Nursing and Community Health Studies, she has used her extensive experience in adult education in her work for the United Kingdom Council for Psychotherapy, where she chaired the Training Standards and Membership Committee of the Psychoanalytic and Psychodynamic Section. In addition to working as an individual psychotherapist, Kate is consultant to, and has run workshops for, a range of community and mental health projects on the themes of attachment and trauma. One of her particular interests is in sibling relationships.

ACKNOWLEDGEMENTS

Thanks to the Bowlby Memorial Conference Planning Group of 2003 and 2004: Wayne Barron, Sarah Benamer, Christine Blake, Richard Bowlby, Sally Forman, Claire Harris, Tori Leach, Penny McMillan, Susie Orbach, Joseph Schwartz, Kate White, Rachel Wingfield, and Judy Yellin, whose hard work and innovatory ideas for the whole project of first producing the conference and now this monograph have enabled it to be accomplished. Thanks especially to Brett Kahr for his vision and unstinting support as well as for generously agreeing to write the Foreword. A big thank you to all the contributors to the conference who agreed to make their papers available for publication.

Finally, and most significantly, thanks to our Tenth John Bowlby Memorial Lecturer 2003, Susie Orbach, for her courage in presenting this ground-breaking work on the body and for her infectious and sustaining enthusiasm for the project which has made it such a success.

Kate White

A personal reminiscence of John Bowlby

Brett Kahr

I first met Dr John Bowlby at approximately 3.00 p.m. on Monday 20th February, 1984, in the courtyard of Corpus Christi College at the University of Oxford. Although I do tend to have a good memory for dates and times, I very much doubt that I could recall the exact temporal coordinates of any other first meeting with so much precision, excepting perhaps one or two intimate family events. But the thrill of meeting the great John Bowlby proved so momentous that details of our encounter remain engraved in the storage cupboards of my long-term memory some two decades hence.

As a postgraduate student in psychology at the University of Oxford, I organized The Oxford Psycho-Analytical Forum, the first psychoanalytical body established under the aegis of the university. During the years in which the society flourished, from 1983 until 1986, many distinguished clinicians and academics accepted our invitation to speak, ranging from Dr Hanna Segal to Dr Ronald Laing. No doubt the allure of lecturing at Great Britain's most ancient university enticed many London psychoanalysts to Oxford and in view of the lack of psychologically orientated arenas in Oxford, the series of talks and conferences proved extremely successful.

After Bowlby's arrival at College, I took him to tea at a restaurant in Broad Street. Bowlby answered all of my eager questions about his life and work with extreme graciousness. Hungry for information about the early history of psychoanalysis in Cambridge, where Bowlby had undertaken his undergraduate studies, I listened with delight as he reminisced instructively about many key figures. For instance, Bowlby proved to be the first person that I had met who was familiar with the life and work of John MacCurdy, a forgotten figure who had helped to pioneer psychoanalysis in the USA before becoming a lecturer at the University of Cambridge and author of arguably the first intelligent critical study of classical psychoanalysis, *Problems in Dynamic Psychology: A Critique of Psychoanalysis and Suggested Forumulations* (MacCurdy, 1923). Bowlby told me that during his studies at the University of Cambridge he had read MacCurdy's later volume, *Common Principles in Psychology and Physiology* (1928). A good intellectual historian of psychoanalysis would do well to trace the impact of this volume upon Bowlby's subsequent work in ethology and attachment.

Bowlby delivered a fine lecture to The Oxford Psycho-Analytical Forum about his work on attachment theory. After the lecture he attended a dinner party I had arranged in his honour with several advanced psychology students as guests. Bowlby told me that he particularly appreciated the opportunity to meet students whose ideas had not yet become ossified, and who would be receptive to new horizons in psychology in a way that might prove impossible for his elder colleagues. Our conversation over dinner covered a wide range of topics, including an appreciation of the links between the work of John Bowlby and that of Erich Fromm, another neglected pioneer of psychoanalysis. As we drove Bowlby from the restaurant to his car, he gave me a preview of his ongoing research on Charles Darwin's symptomatology, and he presented a very persuasive argument that Darwin's neurosis (contrary to the assertions of the voluble biologist Sir Peter Medawar) resulted not from an infestation acquired during his *Beagle* voyage, but rather as a result of unresolved mourning following the death of his mother.

Bowlby had a great impact on literally thousands of workers in the psychoanalytical and psychotherapeutic fields, including John Southgate, one of the founders of the Centre for Attachment-based

Psychoanalytic Psychotherapy (CAPP), who had undergone clinical supervision with Bowlby. I suggested that, as so many of the people in CAPP had enjoyed such uniquely positive experiences with Bowlby, we ought to inaugurate an annual John Bowlby Memorial Lecture. John Southgate and Kate White instantly recognized the merit in this suggestion, and, with great creativity, CAPP took up the challenge of organizing the first John Bowlby Memorial Lecture in 1994, presented by Bowlby's colleague Dr Colin Murray Parkes, our leading authority on the psychiatry of grief and mourning.

Oliver Rathbone of Karnac Books responded very warmly to our suggestion that the John Bowlby Memorial Lectures should now be published as a separate monograph series. Under the editorship of Kate White, CAPP can now present the highlights of the annual memorial conferences in published form, to be read by professionals and students in our field as a permanent record of new work in the disciplines of attachment and psychoanalysis.

The Tenth John Bowlby Memorial Conference

The proceedings of The Tenth John Bowlby Memorial Conference on "Touch: Attachment and the Body", held in London on 7–8 March 2003, provide us with a comprehensive account of a much neglected topic, touch, in all its manifestations, both physical and emotional, as it relates to the developmental process and to the psychoanalytical process. The cornerstone of the conference papers, the John Bowlby Memorial Lecture delivered by Professor Susie Orbach, offers a new and path-breaking theory of the body, and of the role of the body in psychoanalytical practice. The papers speak for themselves, with excellent additional contributions by Ms Anne Aiyegbusi, Ms Margot Sunderland, and Professor Colwyn Trevarthen, along with a rich array of appendices describing the history of the John Bowlby Memorial Lecture, as well as a summary of the small group discussions on the crucial topic of body countertransference. Sadly, the contribution of Ms Pat Cohen could not be included for reasons of confidentiality, but those of us who attended the conference will remember her moving account of her work with an exceptionally traumatized individual, and how this impacted bodily upon her. The range of professional backgrounds

of the speakers—child psychotherapist, psychotherapist, psychoan-
alyst, developmental psychologist, psychiatric nurse—testifies to
the breadth and open-mindedness of the discussion.

The Centre for Attachment-based Psychoanalytic Psychotherapy stands as one of the most pioneering organizations in the
British psychoanalytical community and the first to place attachment and relationality at the centre of the clinical encounter. For this
reason Sir Richard Bowlby, Chair of the Trustees of CAPP, has
always regarded the work of CAPP as the logical extension of his
father's legacy.

Much maligned by orthodox psychoanalysts in his lifetime,
Bowlby's research and clinical observations on the importance of
attachment, relationality, separation, loss, and mourning, have now
become cornerstones of the psychoanalytical process, both nation-
ally and internationally. The John Bowlby Memorial Lecture series
provides testament to the changing emphasis in psychoanalysis
and psychotherapy from the interpretation of the transference as
the crucial vehicle for clinical change to that of a secure-enough
base in the therapeutic relationship (of which transference interpretation may feature as a component). Clinicians practising within the
attachment-based relational tradition have pioneered work with the
most traumatized individuals, whether those suffering from the
long-term sequelae of sexual abuse or from other severe injuries,
both physical and emotional. I look forward to a long association
between CAPP and Karnac Books, so that the fruits of the John
Bowlby Memorial Lecture and the John Bowlby Memorial
Conference can be shared by colleagues in decades to come.

Brett Kahr
1st January, 2004.

REFERENCES.

MacCurdy, John T. (1923). *Problems in Dynamic Psychology: A Critique
    of Psychoanalysis and Suggested Formulations*. New York:
    Macmillan Company.
MacCurdy, John T. (1928). *Common Principles in Psychology and
    Physiology*. London: Cambridge University Press.

Attachment theory and The John Bowlby Memorial Lecture: a short history

Bernice Laschinger

The first John Bowlby Memorial Lecture, given in 1994 by Colin Murray Parkes, focused on bereavement and loss, appropriate themes for the occasion. It is fitting that this year's Bowlby Memorial Lecture, the tenth, should recognize the centrality of the place of the body within the matrix of relational theory and practice. Although the body has been undertheorized in attachment theory, it has always been implicit. Its central source of motivation has been the child's need for proximity to the body of the mother. It is also true to say that the basic premises of attachment theory have powerfully influenced the infancy and neuroscience research which have fuelled so much of the current interest in the relational body. This research has demonstrated the critical role of physical interactions between care-giver and child in feeding, soothing, and handling in shaping the experience of self and other.

The theme of the body thus links to the origins of attachment theory. As a teacher of deprived children and later as a child psychiatrist, John Bowlby became powerfully aware of the longing of young children for the physical presence of their care-givers and of their corresponding traumatic experiences of separation and loss. These perceptions laid the empirical foundations of the theory.

Bowlby's post-war studies of refugee children led to the publication of his seminal work, *Maternal Care and Mental Health* by the World Health Organization in 1952. (Bowlby, 1952). He also studied children in hospital and a residential nursery, in conjunction with James Robertson, who filmed them. The documented sequence of the children's responses to separation in terms of protest, detachment, and despair provided evidence of separation anxiety. The impact of these ideas on the development of child-care policy has been enormous. The 2001 Bowlby Memorial Lecturer, Michael Rutter, dealt with institutional care and the role of the state in promoting recovery from neglect and abuse. His lecture was a testament to the continuing relevance of Bowlby's thinking to contemporary social issues.

Although Bowlby joined the British Psychoanalytic Society in the 1930s and received his training from Joan Riviere and Melanie Klein, he became increasingly sceptical of their focus on the inner fantasy life of the child rather than the way real life experience became internalized, and tended towards what would now be termed a relational approach. Thus, in searching for a theory which could explain the anger and distress of separated young children, Bowlby turned to disciplines outside psychoanalysis, such as ethology. He became convinced of the relevance of animal, and particularly primate, behaviour to our understanding of the normal process of attachment. These relational concepts presented a serious challenge to the closed world of psychoanalysis in the 1940s, and earned Bowlby the hostility of his erstwhile colleagues for several decades.

The maintenance of physical proximity by a young animal to a preferred adult is found in a number of animal species. This suggested to Bowlby that attachment behaviour has a survival value, the most likely function of which is that of care and protection, particularly from predators. It is activated by conditions such as sickness, fear and fatigue. The threat of loss leads to anxiety and anger; actual loss to anger and sorrow. When efforts to restore the bond fail, attachment behaviour may diminish, but will persist at an unconscious level and may become reactivated by reminders of the lost adult, or new experiences of loss.

Attachment theory's basic premise is that, from the beginning of life, the baby human has a primary need to establish an emotional bond with a caregiving adult. Attachment is seen as a source of human motivation as fundamental as those of food and sex. Bowlby postulated that

> Attachment behaviour is any form of behaviour that results in a person attaining or maintaining proximity to some other preferred and differentiated individual. . . . While especially evident during early childhood, attachment behaviour is held to characterize human beings from the cradle to the grave. [Bowlby, 1979, p. 129]

Attachment theory highlights the importance of mourning in relation to trauma and loss. An understanding of the relevance of this to therapeutic practice was a vital element in the foundation of The Centre for Attachment-based psychoanalytic Psychotherapy (CAPP). The consequences of disturbed and unresolved mourning processes was a theme taken up by Colin Murray Parkes when he gave the first John Bowlby Memorial Lecture in 1994.

Mary Ainsworth, an American psychologist who became Bowlby's lifelong collaborator, established the inter-connectedness between attachment behaviour, care-giving in the adult, and exploration in the child. While the child's need to explore, and the need for proximity might seem contradictory, they are in fact complementary. It is the mother's provision of a secure base, to which the child can return after exploration, which enables the development of self-reliance and autonomy. Ainsworth developed the Strange Situation Test for studying individual differences in the attachment patterns of young children. She was able to correlate these to their mother's availability and responsiveness. Her work provided both attachment theory and psychoanalysis with empirical support for some basic premises. This gave the necessary link between attachment concepts and their application to individual experience in a clinical setting.

Over the last two decades the perspective of attachment theory has been greatly extended by the work of Mary Main, who was another Bowlby Memorial Lecturer. She developed the Adult Attachment Interview in order to study the unconscious processes which underlie the behavioural pattern of attachment identified by Mary Ainsworth. Further support came from the perspective of infant observation and developmental psychology developed by yet another Bowlby Memorial Lecturer, Daniel Stern. The lecturer for 2000, Allan Schore, presented important developments in the new field of neuro-psychoanalysis describing emerging theories of how attachment experiences in early life shape the developing brain.

The links between attachment theory and psychoanalysis have also been developed. Josephine Klein, a great supporter of CAPP and also a former contributor to the annual conference, has explored these links in psychotherapeutic practice. In particular, the 1998 Bowlby Memorial Lecturer, Stephen Mitchell, identified a paradigm shift away from drive theory within psychoanalysis. His proposed "relational matrix" links attachment theory to other relational psychoanalytic theories which find so much resonance in the current social and cultural climate. Within this area of convergence, between attachment research and developmental psychoanalysis, the 1999 Bowlby Lecturer, Peter Fonagy, has developed the concept of "mentalization", extending our understanding of the importance of the reflective function, particularly in adversity.

In similar vein, the work of Beatrice Beebe, last year's Lecturer, represents another highly creative development in the unfolding relational narrative of the researcher–clinician dialogue. Her unique research has demonstrated how the parent–infant interaction creates a distinct system organized by mutual influence and regulation which are reproduced in the adult therapeutic relationship.

In the movement to bring the body into the forefront of relational theory and practice, this year's Bowlby Memorial Lecturer, Susie Orbach, a CAPP Trustee, has been a leading pioneer. It was the publication of her ground-breaking books, *Fat is a Feminist Issue* and *Hunger Strike* which introduced a powerful and influential approach to the study of the body in its social context. Her subsequent work, drawing on a convergence of feminism and object relations, extensively expanded and elaborated on these original insights from a psychoanalytic perspective. Over the last decade, one of her major interests has been the construction of sexuality and bodily experience and how these themes play out in the therapeutic relationship. In this she powerfully demonstrates that two persons in relation are two bodies in relation.

References

Bowlby, J. (1952). *Maternal Care and Mental Health* (2nd edn), World Health Organisation: Monograph Series, No. 2. Geneva: World Health Organisation.

Bowlby, J. (1979). *The Making and Breaking of Affectional Bonds.* London: Tavistock.

Introduction to the John Bowlby Memorial Conference 2003

Touch: attachment and the body

Kate White

This is the Tenth John Bowlby Memorial Conference. The planning group who put this conference together used this introductory statement as their starting point.

The significance of the body and bodily experience is crucial in our psychological worlds. This conference explores our thinking about the developmental, relational and interpersonal aspects of the body. We have invited lead researchers and clinicians to discuss ways in which physical communications, body countertransferences, the somatic, and the neural are experienced and expressed in the therapeutic encounter. The conference has been planned to be informative and provocative, exploring the subject of touch, which has become a taboo area within psychoanalytic psychotherapy.

As a starting point for tonight it seems appropriate that we bring our theme into the room and connect through touch. I invite you to shake hands with two people, preferably one who you know and one who you don't. Introduce yourself by name. Notice your bodily responses in this relatively commonplace experience of touch and how much you are aware of touch, the feel of your skin, the visuals, and the sound made by your voice. Reflect for a moment on the *difference you feel in your body* now to the moment before. For those of you who would rather not, this activity is not compulsory.

Perhaps relational approaches to psychoanalytic psychotherapy have underplayed the central role of the body in constructing experience and the shaping of our internal worlds. The child's longing for the body of the mother has always been implicit in attachment theory. Yet perhaps in reaction to the excesses of certain classical theories, and because of its need to achieve scientific respectability, the body and by implication touch, the sexual and the erotic have been undertheorized. Like other relational theories attachment theory has been criticized for its tendencies to desexualize and sanitize.

What is central to relational practice is our understanding that affect and meaning-making emerges through relationship. In the past decade, buttressed by infancy research and neuroscience, the relational body has moved to the foreground. Here the basic premise is that the self is first and foremost an *intersubjective bodily self in a social matrix and cultural setting*. How the infant eats and is fed, how its states of distress and anxiety and desire are recognized, regulated, understood or ignored becomes part of the experience of self and other which is encoded in the body.

Freud's famous adage was that "the ego is first and foremost a bodily ego". Conversely we can understand that the body is a social and cultural body.

The most powerful therapeutic metaphors for problematic adult sexuality discussed in the study group at The Centre for Attachment-based Psychoanalytic Psychotherapy (CAPP) on this subject were found to be derived from the child's experience as an object in the power of her parents. They can do what they wish with the body of the baby—be gentle and loving or invasive, intrusive, harsh, and cruel in their touch. The baby is their product and possession.

We recognize how powerfully these themes are replayed in therapy. Unmediated by language, compelling unconscious communications emerge in body sensations and feelings, in forms of visual contact, of breathing, of sounds, touch, body postures, and even clothes. Most of these take their significance from the other.

Here the relational idea of therapy as an intersubjective encounter can come into play. Through extending the understanding of non-verbal meanings, counter-transference provides a powerful guide to the mysteries of the non-verbal body in that access to these meanings can only be discovered through our capacity to access our own subjective feelings and bodily states. This can feel an overwhelming task. It opens us up to the frailty of our own bodies, our own fears of invasion, and the riskiness of our own erotic desires.

While cognisant of the danger, it is these risks that offer transformational therapeutic opportunities. Erotic transference and counter-transference feelings have the effect of taking us through known and predictable therapeutic territory. For example, the experience of wanting to sensually hold a client, as one might apparently do to a loved child, or having erotic feelings as with a lover, or with a teenager showing off sexually, takes the therapeutic relationship into a new dimension and lends an intensity to the therapeutic experience.

We hope that this conference will provide you with the opportunity to explore the complex and interwoven themes of touch, attachment and the body and their emergence in clinical work. In the different sessions we will consider the impact of difference within the theme under discussion and think about the impact of power, trauma and oppression on the development of the body and its implications for touch in the therapeutic context.

As you will see, the programme for this conference is developmental in its four-part structure. So, colleagues, I invite you to become participants with us on the developmental pathway of this conference as we explore the theme of "Touch: attachment and the body".

Intimate contact from birth

How we know one another by touch, voice, and expression in movement

Colwyn Trevarthen

The discovered baby

All philosophies and sciences, especially the teaching and medical sciences concerned with changing human states, "invent" explanations of the human nature they presume to deal with. They project their intellectual and practical concerns into an image of what is essential in our actions and experience, what biology and psychology is there to start with, and what can change. They make up ideas about the beginning infant consciousness, mostly describing its limitations. I think psychoanalysis, and attachment theory, too, has invented the infant mind.

Recently something new has happened. Research methods have been found to "discover" what infants truly can do and know, and how they feel about it. The findings by careful observation and more receptive experiment can change our understanding of human needs, and of how to care for illnesses of the body and mind.

I will review discoveries about the efforts infants make to find joy and pride in agreeable human company, how a young child's intuition seeks to share adventures of the body in action, triumphing in discovery of others' meaning, and in showing this intelligence. My aim will be to cast light on the deep needs of human beings for making contact with one another, both intimately and in more casual sociable ways, through the rhythm and power of moving. I want to explain why I find that companionship in liveliness and experience is something more than attachment for protection. I want to illuminate the inner "spirit" of the child between body and mind—what comes from inside as exuberance, inspiration, enthusiasm, and what is received as encouragement. The infant's vitality needs more than comfort, holding, security, and nourishment. It fears more than discomfort, hunger, and pain. It fears loneliness, lack of sympathy, and shame. It needs other persons to give and receive knowledge and skill, all that the human imagination and thought can create and use.

I believe developmental psychology has finally proved what is obvious to common sense; that we are born to live as a character in a community of characters, making art, myths, and cultural history, that our spirit needs stories and storytellers, that we have an innate "communicative musicality" that responds to the touches, sights and sounds of human bodies intending and feeling "emotional" about the rewards and risks inseparable from acting and inventing in human company. I summarize this as a theory of "companionship".

Who is a companion?

A parent, grandparent, brother, or sister who shares a baby's pleasure in acting, knowing, and doing, is more than a protector. He or she is a friend—a "companion in adventure"', as the Italians say, who reflects delight in discovery and achievement, and who gives meaning to the baby's natural pride in "making sense". With a stranger, who will probably not know what the baby can do and what he or she likes to share, who seems not to make sense, indeed seems to be "stupid", the baby may immediately seem worried, and soon look away and cry for a familiar face.

An infant's feelings of gratitude and "pride" in the company of someone who gives admiration generously, with love, and the baby's signs of unhappiness or "shame" when there is a chance that he or she will not be understood or liked, are emotions that guide our sympathies and growth of self-confidence through life. These and other "complex relational emotions" are what make human society glad to cooperate and achieve fine, ambitious things. They make us prone to fear or anger when an uncomprehending alien presence or system of belief threatens the common understanding. They can drive the mechanical hubris of enterprise that puts commerce out of touch with nature and simple community needs, or that seeks to impose its blind will by force of political power and arms. That is why a forgiving humility has to be a matter of religious belief, to counter incomprehension, envy, and the want of vengeance.

Gradually the circle of a child's friends expands—even a six-month-old, at the same time as being wary of the stranger, can make generous advances, to "make friends". But the steady growth of pleasure in the company of those a child understands best, and who offer their understanding with enthusiasm and consideration, requires some stability in family and community, as well as in the ways of play and work. Not many children are strong enough in spirit to thrive when all is changing, including the family relationships "at home", the place where every-day meanings should be shared easily and confidently.

I believe it is important to distinguish the emotions that cause a distressed young child to cry for help and comfort from an "attachment figure", and to become calm with affectionate holding, from the exuberant joy of shared play with ways of doing and discovering. I think the emotions of companionship—pride of achievement and shame when sympathy is withdrawn—are important from birth, not learned by socialization, and I conclude they must not be neglected in policies and practices to protect children's emotional health. They are the feelings that open the door to knowledge and skills, which can only be learned, in "cooperative understanding".

The intricacy of contact and relating at different levels of intimacy

From the start of life, a new-born infant moves to communicate "interest", which is more than pleasure and pain in the body—as if to share feelings, impulses to act, and ideas that are generated from inside, in the mind. Face, voice, hands, the whole body, display the dynamic impulses of seeking for conscious awareness and for testing changes in reality "outside". The acting is coordinated with "future sense" in one time and space defined by the baby's moving body—thus the infant shows to us it has a "self" that intends.

This Self is looking and listening for the vital will and imagination of the Other, not just receiving bodily comfort in the rhythms and accents of immediate body contact. A new-born may imitate expressions of an adult's motives and emotions within minutes of birth. This "mirroring" has been proved to be expectant, purposeful, and reciprocal, and to be coupled to inner physiological states of purposeful energy or still expectancy, the beats of the heart being the tell-tale message of an inner life that prepares for acting.

New-borns use all their senses, some more effectively than others, to perceive what lies behind the movements of another human body. Even a prematurely born infant can, if approached with sufficient gentleness and attention, interact within rhythmic sounds and gestures in time with the adult's vocalizations, touches, and expressions of face or hands, taking turns with the evenly spaced and emotionally enhanced movements. The baby seems to be joining in a musical improvisation of sound and gesture, "swinging" like a naturally skilled jazz musician. The motives that make the baby so expressive with the eyes, the voice, and the hands recognize the signs that other persons are interested. A happy baby enjoys "showing off" how clever he or she is, and receiving due praise from the sympathy of the adult's response.

The scientific demonstration, in the 1960s, of "conversational" abilities in infants six to twelve weeks old paved the way for acceptance that human mental development begins with anticipation of shared experience through rhythmic mirroring of expressive movements. The infant's bold yet sensitive emotions excite parents and others, young or old, to respond. They advertise the baby's spirit of joint adventure, a spirit that will stay important through life, and this early search for company develops rapidly in friendly games where affectionate teasing keeps everyone guessing, and provokes laughter.

Talk with the body is guided by both practical and moral feelings

Two-month-olds attend to a parent's affectionate talk, and respond, and babies as young as six months can share another person's interest in objects and doing things with them, not just emotions related to regulation of visceral states or levels of arousal and excitement. They quickly learn rituals of baby songs and action games, anticipating the "narrative" of activity and sharing episodes of excitement, rising and coming to rest. By one year the baby is showing, by pointing, handling, and vocalizing, that he or she grasps the special interest of many practical things—including the use of peculiar cultural tools like books, cell phones, shoes, cars, and keyboards—and is proud when this knowledge is praised.

Such findings give a new importance to Daniel Stern's "relational emotions", the intricate blends and transitions of expression that affect the way a person relates to changing consciousness of themselves in a companion. It opens a new chapter to the story of human needs for sympathetic relationships, which must carry implications for how children learn to understand the culture and traditions of their parents' world, and the "mother tongue", and how socio-emotional disorders, especially those affecting the infant or young child, can interfere with learning, and how they may be understood and treated.

Being an actor with something to boast about

By six months infants are usually lively playmates. They enjoy games that involve predicting what someone else may do next, and they like teasing and being teased in these games. They start to laugh when other people act in comical ways, and they enjoy others laughing at what they do. All these behaviours lead parents to feel that the baby is becoming more self-aware, more a social personality. Studies of the emotional expression of infants in play indicate that their feelings are much more complex and sensitive than psychologists have believed. The usual theory of how emotions develop from simple sensations of pleasure or displeasure now seems inadequate. For example a two-month-old can show coyness in front of a mirror, and a six-month-old can demonstrate "pride" in showing a favourite trick, such as clapping hands or making a silly noise, or "shame" when a stranger seems not to understand. These are emotions that immediately affect other persons, causing them to react to the baby in helpful or unhelpful ways, which resemble what we go through in more elaborate social negotiations in adult society.

In this period of growing sociability, the infant is also discovering a lot about objects, alerting to their sounds, chasing them with eyes, reaching to catch and grasp them, fingering and mouthing them to test their properties, manipulating and combining them in different ways. This practical, objective intelligence has been given much attention by psychologists since Jean Piaget devised his famous tests of the development of the "object concept"'. Henri Wallon's studies in France of the behaviours that give evidence of "person concepts" and social awareness, contemporary with those of Piaget, have largely been overlooked in the English-speaking world.

In 1974, one of my colleagues, Penelope Hubley, discovered that a baby she was following closely, week by week, suddenly became very attentive to what her mother was doing with objects, and ready for the first time to follow looks and pointing to take up an instruction from the mother about what to do with things they were playing with. Further work has proved that this change, at about nine months after birth, is a very important development. We called it the development of "secondary intersubjectivity" or "person–person–object" awareness. (Trevarthen & Hubley, 1978). With it, the baby becomes a good pupil, interested in learning by watching other people and listening and looking when they make suggestions of what to do. Soon the baby is learning meanings at a great rate, and trying to know things and perform learned skills like other familiar persons. Everything people do or use becomes a topic of interest. The baby has become a pupil, and this causes others to be teachers. The road to culture and all its artificial meanings and uses is open.

Steps to making sense

Observation of age-related changes in infants' skills and preferences, through infancy and toddlerhood to culture-related "imaginative" (story-making) play and language, shows that every advance in the infant's interests and powers of moving also transforms emotional communication with attentive parents and with siblings. The baby's growing inventiveness and sense of fun affects everyone's attempts to gain playful reactions until, by the end of the first year, he or she is expected to be an alert and cheerful partner in many recognized games and collaborative activities, and to have interesting ideas of how to do things. A sequence of behaviours has been defined by descriptive research that display the unique human capacity for generating and learning arbitrary meanings by joint purposeful and cooperative interest in objects and situations. It has become clear that the toddler's motives for joint interest with companions in the common world is no less than the key to language learning, both declarative identification of objects or actions of interest and narrative cohesion in social and mimetic fantasy play being thoroughly mastered nearly a year before any words are used.

A one-year-old toddler's attentiveness and willing acceptance of new ideas and new skills, including theatrical skills like dancing and singing, invites older, more experienced companions to teach. It also stimulates persons of all ages to become childish again—simply exuberant. Formal and informal education both depend upon the child's motives or "disposition" to learn, as much as upon adults' wish to teach. Early learning needs no "curriculum" that sets targets for teaching and that counts achievements. The creativity and curiosity of children are sensitive to the manner of teaching, which defines the quality of friendship in "collaborative learning". Shared discovery prepares the ground for further investigations of what can be learned together—and they sustain interest when the investigating child is alone, supported by memories of favourite teachers.

When reflections between minds are distorted

The theory of "innate intersubjectivity" claims that human beings are equipped at birth with abilities and feelings prepared for sympathetic and cooperative mental life in a society that creates meanings, seeks to be governed by them, and transmits them to the young. The primary aim of this development appears to be to sustain mutually supportive companionship in experience and purposes, thus preparing the way to a life in a community with its inventions and history. The pleasure we feel in being successful in what we do, and the shame or sadness we feel if we fail to come up to others' expectations have their origins in the motives of very young children to understand the world in the company of the people they know best.

These motives and emotions can develop pathology. Infants can have disorders of psychological regulation, and of imagining objects and persons, as happens, for example, in autism. Failure of the primary motive mechanisms of the mind will have effects that may be very difficult in the future life of the child, adolescent, and adult, and very worrying for their family. To understand how problems of psychological development can be caused, and how they might be responded to sensitively in therapy or education, we need an accurate idea of what the infant's motives are normally adapted to do in transactions with the outside world. Most of all, we must know how a baby understands, and is understood by, other human beings; how they become companions in discovery and adventure, before the mind has any words.

Tests of a young infant's motives and feelings in communicating

The most challenging evidence for two-month-olds acting with feeling and knowing what should happen next has come from two kinds of experiment that test young babies' awareness of the "contingency" or responsiveness of a parent's expressions in communication. In proto-conversations, adult and infant join in rhythmic patterns of moving, exchanging sounds, face expressions, or gestures with predictable regularity, sometimes synchronizing, but more often alternating with a regular timing. These patterns appear to be created by both infant and adult, each accurately predicting what the other will do. We can test the baby's reactions to see if there are any signs of disappointment or annoyance when the mother's reply to each utterance is interfered with or "perturbed". Indeed, infants react with clear avoidance and negative emotions when the mother's behaviour is not sensitive in time and sympathetic in feeling.

The first test requires the mother to interrupt her talking and for one minute to look at the baby still and expressionless. This "still face" or "blank face" test causes a two-month-old to stop smiling and vocalizing happily, stare, look away, and show feelings of confusion, sadness, or annoyance. The second experiment used television inter-communication. Mother and infant are placed in separate rooms where each can see a TV image of the other and hear the other's voice. A two-month-old can communicate well with the mother if the set-up has dimensions that enable the image of the mother to be close to that a baby normally sees when she is holding the baby in front of her. Then a portion of a happy proto-conversation is replayed to the baby, with all its lively expressions intact. Because the replayed image has no awareness, it cannot respond to anything the baby does. The baby quickly detects this and reacts with distress and avoidance, much as in the still face experiment. These two experiments prove that a young baby is very sensitive to a lack of sympathetic and "live" response from the mother.

Further evidence of a baby's active awareness of how a parent is responding, and of the emotional feeling that is being shown by the parent, comes from research on infants' reactions to the arrhythmic and tuneless talking of a depressed mother who is finding it very difficult to perceive her baby as a sympathetic person. A depressed mother's detached or intrusive way of addressing her baby causes the baby to avoid her, which only makes things worse. Sometimes the baby becomes chronically depressed, too. This can reduce the baby's chances of developing a normal curiosity and interest in learning. In other words, failure of emotional support can lead the baby to lose some of his or her capacity for doing and knowing. Cognitive development is affected by a loss of communication.

These observations prove that young infants are counting on emotionally appropriate responses from a parent, that they are sensitive to the effects of what they themselves do, and that they can perceive the relevance of what the other person does. Theories that assume an infant has first to discover the effects of moving his or her own body before detecting another person's body movements, by learning the time relations of stimulation received as feed-back, say that this degree of awareness is impossible at this age. It is assumed, from studies of eye–hand coordination and behaviours in an apparatus that reacts to the infant's limb movements, to be a skill that an infant takes several months to construct. The perturbation tests, and other demonstrations of purposeful actions by new-borns, show that being able to anticipate consequences of moving is a psychological function that a human being is born with, a use of time in the mind to find the mind in another person. It is also clear that this ability is crucial in developing a relationship by communicating with another person who is a sympathetic companion.

The theory of therapy without words

The communications of infants show that we are born sensitive to the rhythms and expressive forms of other persons' movements, which carry affecting messages. These inborn abilities explain why therapists who make no attempt to persuade or remind patients verbally, and who do not require the patient to make any conscious cognitive appraisal of their feelings and behaviour, can gain the confidence of patients of any age. They indicate how intimate non-verbal communication can help resolve psycho-affective problems and confusion of understanding, rebuilding confidence by supporting the inner motives for discovery in communication.

The non-verbal therapist, employing music, art, dance, or touch-and-movement techniques, stimulates and supports impulses and feelings of human contact, and this can change a patient's emotional experiences and motives to communicate. All humans can feel rhythmic impulses and affective qualities that echo their own expressions in time and emotional quality. Changes in motivation and emotion mediated by sympathetic communication and responding to the expressions of a partner in action and awareness can evoke improvements in motor coordination, cognitive alertness, discrimination, learning, and thinking. Communication can change the neuro-affective state of a person's brain.

Non-verbal communication, including improvised music and movement and touch therapies, can help a variety of disorders affecting a young child's relating, including: autism, ADHD, distressed infants born very prematurely and in intensive care, severely mentally handicapped and deaf–blind children, language impairment, and maternal post-natal depression.

A rational/cognitive psychology emphasizing categorical awareness and thinking, or one that depends on a cultivated literary interpretation of consciousness as if it were entirely built of the meanings of words, cannot easily explain how movement therapy or music therapy can be beneficial. Intellectual approaches to psychotherapy often assume that emotional life is constructed in early childhood, and that conflicts and emotional disorders result from negative experiences that bring fear, pain, and guilt into the simple emotional life of the child. Nevertheless, infants can communicate with sensitivity and precision, and they can powerfully influence the affects and motivation of adults. They clearly have complex affective states and are aware of such states in other persons.

I am sure therapists need a model of non-verbal communication based upon acceptance of intrinsic affective states and their communication by active contact between bodies in all degrees of intimacy.

References

Adamson, L. B. (1996). *Communication and Development During Infancy.* Boulder, CO: Westview Press.

Beebe, B., & Lachmann, F. M. (2002). *Infant Research and Adult Treatment: Co-Constructing Interactions.* Hillsdale, NJ: The Analytic Press.

Bråten, S. (1998). Intersubjective communion and understanding: Development and perturbation. In: S.Bråten (Ed.), *Intersubjective Communication and Emotion in Early Ontogeny* (pp. 372–382). Cambridge: Cambridge University Press.

Bruner, J. S. (1996). *The Culture of Education.* Cambridge, MA: Harvard University Press.

Custodero, L., & Fenichel, E. (Eds.) (2002). The musical lives of babies and families. *Zero to Three, 23*(1).

Dissanayake, E. (2000). *Art and Intimacy: How the Arts Began.* Seattle and London: University of Washington Press.

Donaldson, M. (1995). *Human Minds: An Exploration.* London: Allen Lane/Penguin Books.

Draghi-Lorenz, R., Reddy, V., & Costall, A. (2001). Re-thinking the development of "non-basic" emotions: A critical review of existing theories. *Developmental Review*, 21(3): 263–304.

Field, T. (1998). Maternal depression effects on infants and early intervention. *Preventative Medicine*, 27, 200–203.

Forman, D. R., & Kochanska, G. (2001). Viewing imitation as child responsiveness: A link between teaching and discipline domains of socialization. *Developmental Psychology*, 37(2): 198–206.

Gratier, M. (1999). Expressions of belonging: the effect of acculturation on the rhythm and harmony of mother–infant vocal interaction. In: *Rhythms, Musical Narrative, and the Origins of Human Communication. Musicae Scientiae, Special Issue, 1999–2000* (pp. 93–122). Liège: European Society for the Cognitive Sciences of Music.

Hobson, P. (2002). *The Cradle of Thought: Exploring the Origins of Thinking*. London: Macmillan.

Kugiumutzakis, G. (1999). Genesis and development of early infant mimesis to facial and vocal models. In: J. Nadel & G. Butterworth (Eds.) *Imitation in Infancy* (pp. 36–59). Cambridge: Cambridge University Press.

Murray, L., & Andrews, L. (2000). *The Social Baby: Understanding Babies' Communication from Birth*. Richmond, Surrey: CP Publishing.

Murray, L., & Cooper, P. J. (Eds.) (1997). *Postpartum Depression and Child Development*. New York: Guilford Press.

Nadel, J., & Pezé, A. (1993). Immediate imitation as a basis for primary communication in toddlers and autistic children. In J. Nadel & L. Camioni (Eds.), *New Perspectives in Early Communicative Development* (pp. 139–156). London: Routledge.

Papousek, M. (1996). Intuitive parenting: A hidden source of musical stimulation in infancy. In: I. Deliège & J. Sloboda (Eds.), *Musical Beginnings: Origins and Development of Musical Competence* (pp. 88–112). Oxford: Oxford University Press.

Reddy, V. (1991). Playing with others' expectations: teasing and mucking about in the first year (pp. 143–158). In: A. Whiten (Ed.), *Natural Theories of Mind*. Oxford: Blackwell.

Reddy, V. (2000). Coyness in early infancy. *Developmental Science*, 3(2): 186–192.

Reddy, V. (2003). Before the 'Third Element': Understanding attention to self. In: N. Eilan, J. Roessler, & P. McCormack (Eds.), *Joint Attention: Perspectives from Philosophy and Psychology*. Oxford: Oxford University Press.

Reddy, V., Hay, D., Murray, L., & Trevarthen, C. (1997). Communication in infancy: Mutual regulation of affect and attention. In: G. Bremner, A. Slater, & G. Butterworth (Eds.), *Infant Development: Recent Advances* (pp. 247–274). Hove, East Sussex: Psychology Press.

Rogoff, B. (1990). *Apprenticeship in Thinking: Cognitive Development in Social Context.* New York: Oxford University Press.

Selby, J. M., & Sylvester Bradley, B. (2003). Infants in groups: A paradigm for the study of early social experience. *Human Development.* (in press).

Stern, D. N. (1993). The role of feelings for an interpersonal self. In: U. Neisser (Ed.), *The Perceived Self: Ecological and Interpersonal Sources of the Self-Knowledge* (pp. 205–215). New York: Cambridge University Press.

Stern, D. N. (2000). *The Interpersonal World of the Infant: A View from Psychoanalysis and Development Psychology.* (2nd edn). New York: Basic Books.

Trehub, S. E. (1990). The perception of musical patterns by human infants: The provision of similar patterns by their parents. In: M. A. Berkley & W. C. Stebbins (Eds.), *Comparative Perception; Vol. 1, Mechanisms* (pp. 429–459). New York: Wiley.

Trevarthen, C. (1993). The function of emotions in early infant communication and development. In: J. Nadel & L. Camaioni (Eds.), *New Perspectives in Early Communicative Development* (pp. 48–81). New York: Routledge.

Trevarthen, C. (1994). Infant semiosis. In: W. Noth (Ed.), *Origins of Semiosis* (pp. 219–252). Berlin: Mouton de Gruyter.

Trevarthen, C. (1995). Contracts of mutual understanding: negotiating meaning and moral sentiments with infants. *Journal of Contemporary Legal Issues, 6:* 373–407.

Trevarthen, C. (1998a). The concept and foundations of infant intersubjectivity. In: S. Bråten (Ed.), *Intersubjective Communication and Emotion in Early Ontogeny.* (pp. 15–46). Cambridge: Cambridge University Press.

Trevarthen, C. (1998b). Explaining emotions in attachment. (Review of Sroufe, L. A. (1996) *Emotional Development: The Organization of Emotional Life in Early Years.* Cambridge: Cambridge University Press.) *Social Development, 7*(2): 269–272.

Trevarthen, C. (1999). Musicality and the intrinsic motive pulse: evidence from human psychobiology and infant communication In: *Rhythms, Musical Narrative, and the Origins of Human Communication.*

Musicae Scientiae, Special Issue, 1999–2000 (pp. 157–213). Liège: European Society for the Cognitive Sciences of Music.

Trevarthen, C. (2001a). Intrinsic motives for companionship in understanding: their origin, development and significance for infant mental health. *International Journal of Infant Mental Health, 22*(1–2): 95–131.

Trevarthen, C. (2001b). The neurobiology of early communication: intersubjective regulations in human brain development. In: A. F. Kalverboer & A. Gramsbergen (Eds.), *Handbook on Brain and Behavior in Human Development,* (pp. 841–882). Dordrecht, The Netherlands: Kluwer Academic Publishers.

Trevarthen, C. (2002a). Origins of musical identity: evidence from infancy for musical social awareness. In: R. MacDonald, D. J. Hargreaves, & D. Miell (Eds.), *Musical Identities* (pp. 21–38). Oxford: Oxford University Press.

Trevarthen, C. (2002b). Learning in companionship. *Education in the North, New Series, No. 10*: 16–25. The University of Aberdeen.

Trevarthen, C. (2003). Making sense of infants making sense. *Intellectica: Revue de l'Association pour la Recherche Cognitive, 1.* Paris (in press)

Trevarthen, C., & Aitken, K. J. (1994). Brain development, infant communication, and empathy disorders: intrinsic factors in child mental health. *Development and Psychopathology, 6*: 597–633.

Trevarthen, C,. & Aitken, K. J. (2001). Infant intersubjectivity: research, theory and clinical applications. *Annual Research Review, Journal of Child Psychology and Psychiatry, 42*(1): 3–48.

Trevarthen, C., & Aitken, K. J. (2003). Regulation of brain development and age-related changes in infants' motives: the developmental function of "regressive" periods. In: M. Heimann & F. Plooij (Eds.), *Regression Periods in Human Infancy* (pp. 107–184). Mahwah, NJ: Erlbaum.

Trevarthen, C., Aitken, K. J., Papoudi, D., & Robarts, J. Z. (1998). *Children with Autism: Diagnosis and Interventions to Meet their Needs* (2nd edn). London: Jessica Kingsley.

Trevarthen, C., & Hubley, P. (1978). Secondary intersubjectivity: confidence, confiding and acts of meaning in the first year. In: A. Lock (Ed.), *Action, Gesture and Symbol* (pp. 183–229). London: Academic Press.

Trevarthen, C. & Malloch, S. (2000). The dance of wellbeing: defining the musical therapeutic effect. *Norwegian Journal of Music Therapy, 9*(2): 3–17.

Trevarthen, C., & Malloch, S. (2002). Musicality and music before three: human vitality and invention shared with pride. *Zero to Three*, *23*(1): 10–18.

Trevarthen, C., Kokkinaki, T., & Fiamenghi, G. A. Jr. (1999). What infants' imitations communicate: with mothers, with fathers and with peers. In: J. Nadel & G. Butterworth (Eds.), *Imitation in Infancy* (pp. 127–185). Cambridge: Cambridge University Press.

Trevarthen, C., Murray, L., & Hubley, P. A. (1981). Psychology of infants. In: J. Davis & J. Dobbing (Eds.), *Scientific Foundations of Clinical Paediatrics* (2nd edn). (pp. 211–274). London: Heinemann.

Tronick, E. Z., & Weinberg, M. K. (1997). Depressed mothers and infants: failure to form dyadic states of consciousness. In: L. Murray & P. J. Cooper, (Eds.), *Postpartum Depression and Child Development* (pp. 54–81). New York: Guilford Press.

Uzgiris, I. C. (1991). The social context of infant imitation. In: M. Lewis & S. Feinman (Eds.), *Social Influences and Socialization in Infancy*, (pp. 215–251). New York: Plenum Press.

The John Bowlby Memorial Lecture 2003

The body in clinical practice

Part One

There is no such thing as a body

Susie Orbach

> Our self is first and foremost a body-as-experienced-being-handled-and held-by-other-self
>
> Lewis Aron (1998)

> Commonsense, though all very well for everyday purposes, is easily confused, even by such simple questions as . . . when you feel a pain in the leg, where is the pain? If you say it is in your head, would it be in your head if your leg had not been amputated? If you say yes, then what reason have you for ever thinking you have a leg?
>
> Bertrand Russell

How much energy did you put into thinking about what you might wear this morning? Or yesterday when you were seeing your patients or clients? Do you have a uniform you grab for, an all purpose work look that minimizes fussing about clothes on a daily basis? Do you wear different clothes for different patients? Has your style changed? Do you wear bright clothes one day, sexy another, elegant or scruffy at other times? Do you fret about your appearance, wonder how you are perceived by your patients, worry lest they comment on the bodily changes you are going through?

What do you think of how I wear my clothes? Of how I move as I talk, of the register my voice occupies, of how I seem in my body? Do you like what you see? Do you feel uncomfortable, think I'm mutton dressed up as lamb? Are you disturbed by my regularly flicking my hair out of my eyes?

Let's go a step further. How does the way in which I am in *my* body affect your feelings about *your* body? Does it make you more or less self-aware? Does my body presence sanction, confirm, disturb, turn you off, overwhelm you? Does it please you? What does it tell you about you and your body and your relation to other bodies?

Doreen

When I opened the door to Doreen, I never quite knew what to expect. A fifty-year-old professional woman, a heterosexual mother of four grown children, roughly 5 foot 9 and of a big build, she would arrive in what I can only describe as incongruous outfits: stilettos and a short, pink, frou-frou frock one day, a manly and rather cheaply cut business suit with elaborately printed silk cravat the next, a pair of tight lycra leggings with a sweatshirt the time after with child-like ribbons in her hair and then, just once in a while, an outfit which was noteworthy for its credibility. None of these costumes quite seem to fit her. There was rather in Doreen a sense of rehearsal of *dramatis persona*. Unlike the multiple personality whose individual *alters* may inhabit different bodies so that their gait and bearing, the tonal qualities of their voice, the facial expressions they use are discrete (Sinason, 2002), Doreen was not so much a multiple person accommodating different bodies in one skin as a woman trying to find a form of clothing and embodiment that could let her be in her body rather than constantly fret and pay attention to it.

Doreen's sartorial extravaganzas were far from giving her recreational pleasure. Her body was clearly out of synch. It seemed she was using her clothing as a kind of key to get the starter motor going on her body but sadly for her, while the engine would turn over exuberantly as though to engage, it would soon splutter and stall as she donned some other outfit which failed to vivify her body. I pictured her going to her wardrobe as though it was a big dressing up box; expectant and hopeful about who she might be that day.

For my part, I began to feel rather tiny. Alice-like (Carrol, 1865), I felt myself grow down and grow in as though I were a miniature. Doreen appeared as a blow-up doll or perhaps I should more accurately say, an overblown, overgrown, blown-up, pretend woman figure such as are sold for sexual purposes on the internet. My diminution was not altogether unpleasant. I went back and forth between feeling teetered over as though I was this little thing underneath her and then sensing my lungs expand to take a metaphorical hearty breath as they were poised to shoot forward to prick and deflate her. She was at once substantial and puffed out, carrying too much water to let her feet sit comfortably in her dainty shoes and yet almost menacingly large and solid.

My body counter-transference with Doreen was a visceral rendition of her early experience of bodies around her being too large and yet not sufficiently robust or stable enough for her to find or develop a body herself from. She *did* feel them teetering over her. She couldn't get them to be in focus and the volatility of the body size I experienced in the counter-transference was a version of the search for a body for herself that could moor itself by finding a place in the physical storm that surrounded her.

Rob

Rob was a forty-eight-year-old man who came to therapy in the middle of a breakdown. His sleep had been disturbed for months and he was in a loop about being anxious about being anxious. A barrister who was required to perform in front of juries and judges, he could only get himself going on a case if he found a love or sexual interest: the barrister for the other side, the plaintiff or defendant, his junior, his solicitor. The sexual interest took the weight of his anxiety which became transformed into pursuit and sexual performance anxiety. In the course of our time together Rob revealed a wide range of sexual activities. He frequented call-girls, picked up prostitutes for dangerous car rendezvous around the King's Cross red-light district, and engaged in consensual sex so close to the edge that it took a great deal on my part to be curious rather than frightened. Indeed of course, I did become frightened. I found myself one day in a perfectly ordinary session suddenly fearful that Rob would rape me. I felt my body being pulled apart and tearing. I was so scared that time held me in a pincer. I became rigid, started to sweat, cursed myself for not having an alarm alert in my room before I could find a way to still my momentary psychosis. After the session, as I replayed the rape scenario occurring in my body, I was stunned at the level of brutality and the visual acuity of a scene of bodily fluids, teeth, and fight coursing through my body.

Rob had talked about "transgressive" sex in a pseudo liberated way during our sessions. His repetitive sexual exploits appeared to both soothe and terrify him. They gave him a sense of being physically rooted and yet driven by physical forces he couldn't control. He welcomed the rush of desire that precipitated a sexual encounter. He described it as feeling more himself, but in detumescence he felt empty, as though in entering into himself he simultaneously vacated himself. With a consideration of the stark physicality of my body counter-transference in my awareness, we could get much further than the formulation that his sexual activity was a vehicle for anxiety. I took the savagery I experienced as a clue to his terror and his search for another body, for a body that could respond, a body that didn't collapse, a body that could meet his body. Rob had never had an experience of embodiment. His subjective sense of his body was staccato with three main modes. Each mode was an attempt for recognition, for a body that could be seen, a body that could be received, a body that could be confirmed either in its sense of okayness or in its sense of being foul.

In court, Rob entered the performing body. He sought in the eyes of the jury who watched him the admiration and pleasure, the acceptance and recognition, that he had failed to see reflected in his parents' eyes when he was growing up. In sexual pursuit he entered the giving body, the body full of love and tenderness, the body he could love for himself because he could be loved by another. In the third mode, the degraded body, the body in the sleaze of a paid sexual encounter or on the sexual edge, he was propelled by a physical force going at the crash barriers, looking for a kind of containment that could meet his body hatred.

In my body counter-transference experience of imagining myself the victim of potential savage rape, I felt I was in a corporeal translation of a famous Winnicottian paradoxical formulation (Winnicott, 1971): the patient needs to destroy the object and the analyst needs to survive the destruction. What became acute for me was engaging with the notion that my body was required to receive Rob's hatred and aggression. I must manage my alarm, to allow myself to be disturbed by him, but not to collapse under that disturbance. Instead I was required to take the challenge to my physical integrity, remain stable, rooted in my own body in order for there to be a body in the room for him.

Rob could only put together a body for himself via a violent encounter with another and yet on-the-edge and dangerous sex failed for him because he had to hold the boundary. He couldn't go the full destructive route. Via my body counter-transference, I think he gave me the chance to enter into the sense of desperation and need for a body which could be destroyed and yet survive.

A challenge to the body as dustbin to the mind

In both of the cases and the many others that I have directly experienced or supervised, I have been pushed to challenge the mentalist preoccupations of the psychoanalytic wing of our profession with its over-evaluation of mind and thinking as a kind of moral superego to feeling and bodies. Bodies in the current psychoanalytic session are adjuncts to mental processes: sometimes they stimulate affects, sometimes they become diseased, sometimes they represent memory—the body as elephant—sometimes they are seen as deeper as more truthful (this would be a Jungian or Reichian notion) or they are seen as a theatre, as Joyce McDougall (1989) does, as a stage on which the troubles of the psyche are acted and inscribed. But mindedness to the body as a body which is speaking for itself and its difficulties is peculiarly absent.

From Freud and Breuer's hysterics onwards to today's patients with disordered eating and body image problems, to those driven to cut their arms, lacerate their stomachs, their breasts, or become Munchausen creators or psychosomatic textbook entries, the body has become as poetry is to prose: a distillation, an encapsulation, a metaphor.

It has become almost everything else but a breathing, living, desiring, body. In the post-Freudian, post-instinctual body along with losing the sexually pursuant body that marauds and must be tamed for civilization and art, we seem to have lost the body *as body* and the body as having *a psychological and developmental history of its own.*

In moving away from the early medicalized situating of psychoanalysis into a theory of mind and clinical practice, the mind has taken supremacy. In the interpersonal, intra-psychic play of our lives, the mind has taken not just the lead role but those of all the supporting cast, leaving the body as a kind of prompt when the lead actors lose their lines.

This curious lock into the mind and mentalism is so powerful that it even flies in the face of the great findings of psychoanalytic research, developmental psychology, and John Bowlby's towering work on attachment theory. In reading Bowlby what becomes immediately apparent is how physical a theory the theory of attachment is. Indeed, if we tilt our lens slightly and think about attachment theory and developmental theory in general, we notice the frequency with which words like proximity, holding, feeding, weaning, motor development, bodies, anal, oral, genital occur, and we probably can also notice how rapidly we translate these words into a picture of the inter-subjective and intra-psychic relationship, the internal object relationship representations of our patients and their relation to us, their inner world and the transference–countertransference enactments and pressures in the room. Rarely do we see these developmental stories as commentary about their physical development and their subjective sense of their bodies. Let me give you an example of what I mean.

The mother–child relationship and the physical body

When I was becoming interested in the aetiology of eating problems in girls and women (Orbach, 1978, 1982, 1986) and thinking about women's psychology and the construction of femininity and the way in which the social requirements of gender inequality shape the mother–daughter relationship, I would reflect on the research that showed that girl babies are breast-fed for a shorter time span than boys, that each feed tended to last less time, that weaning was more rapid, that potty training was introduced earlier, and that girls were held less than boys (Brunet & Lezine, 1966). I saw these as examples of the very visible dynamics in that mother–daughter relationship (Eichenbaum & Orbach, 1982, 1986; Orbach, 1978) that constructed a femininity that was arced by emotional deprivation and a consequent feeling of unentitlement, a psychic receptivity to second-class citizenship. I would evaluate such material as it occurred in my patients and in the general psychological and psychoanalytic literature as evidence for the internalization of the denial of dependency and the thwarting of autonomy visible in the feminine psychic structure (Chodorow, 1978; Eichenbaum & Orbach, 1983).

I still believe this to be a valid approach but what it misses, or rather what it collapses, under the rubric of the psyche is the significance of the physical treatment of the girl's body and its impact on the development of her subjective sense of her body. I missed understanding how the precise details of physical handling and care affected how the baby girl came to feel in her body and the ways in which the mother's gender-specific treatment of her baby girls and baby boys affected, not just their psychological sense of self, but their *physical* sense of self and their *physical subjective sense of self*. I missed realizing that our body, her body, is a relational body. We learn about it, not all by ourselves "naturally". This is a fiction. There is no more a "natural" body than there is a "natural" psychology. Our body, like our psychic properties and potentialities, emerges out of the emotional ambience and bodily interaction with our care-givers. Our personal body unfolds and develops its individuality in the context of its relationship to and with an other and other bodies.

When I began to look at the powerful body counter-transferences occurring for me with certain people, I started to re-evaluate the dynamics of reading bodily symptoms whether they be eczema, eating problems, colitis, backache, and my bodily counter-transferences, and to see what we might understand if we went beyond interpreting symptoms as states of mind, but more as representing the struggle of the body to come to therapy and to come into being.

While the body as symbol is a rich part of psychoanalysis there are limitations when psychoanalytic therapies can only take bodily symptoms and turn them exclusively into statements about the mind's inability to contain the uncontainable. These uncontainable contents of mind are then seen to be visited on this object or perhaps part object, the body, so that eczema, for example, becomes understood as a physical concretatization of mental prickliness and as a psychic eruption which forces the patient to pick at him or herself.

The body as body

With an open mind to what that eczema *feels* like if I imagine it occurring on my arms or tummy or legs or fingers, I begin to expand my repertoire and to extend beyond the idea of the mind's prickliness to include the notion that the eczema might be the body's prickliness, the body's attempt to insist upon its presence: to announce itself as a body that weeps, a body that itches, a body that is in discomfort. A body whose casing and interface between inner and outer corporeality is somehow compromised. A body that is in need of attention. A body that is not exclusively a vehicle for the mind but a *body searching to become*. A body that needs another body in the room to deconstruct itself and to remake itself.

As psychotherapists we are accustomed to, and comfortable with, the idea that our patients use our psyches as external psyches, as containers and holders when they feel shaky, when they are in the process of deconstructing their defence structures. We see that we become a kind of auxiliary psyche which is robust and flexible enough to manage some of the very terrifying anxieties that ensue when an individual is in the process of dissolving known ways of being. In that process we often experience ourselves as being capable and competent. The sense of a self with a psychological stability we are able to use in the fifty-minute session can be far more contained, alive, sensitive and, in a sense, emotionally healthy during that period. In practising our craft, the technical skills of reflection, self scrutiny, commitment to hearing the other, to take what we receive, and in particular to ponder before spontaneously responding to heavily charged material, is what the patient requires of us and without much noticing it in the counter-transference that is what occurs; we do manage to provide a steady external psyche that can be used by the other.

Patients with very troubled bodies have been able to invoke in me a parallel sense of my body's reliability and steadiness which can then act as a temporary external body for them. In the case of Doreen, when I could recover from the Alice-like volatility, I could use my body counter-transference as a way to help her deconstruct the stabs she kept making to get a body through her diverse sartorial engagements. Working together we could help her face the profound difficulty with embodiment and the sense of not having a body that lay at the core of her body uncertainty.

Doreen was both fussed over and neglected. The awkwardness of her dress sense enunciated this combination. Her body was not yet grown up or grown into. At the same time it was too big for her and prematurely overgrown. Doreen's mother was neglectful of her own body, sleeping at odd times, living off cigarettes and irregular meals, and failed to attend to Doreen's developmental and daily bodily needs. As a child, Doreen would go to sleep at night and when her bandleader father returned from his work after midnight she would wake up to be with him as he chilled out with whisky and story-telling. Doreen would eventually fall asleep next to him.

One might, without the body counter-transference as a guide, be led to alight on sexual misconduct as the explanation for her clothing confusions and interpret her outfits as the child, the wife, the secret oedipal victor, and so on. But, taking seriously the body counter-transference, I was led to consider the rather more fundamental problem that had faced Doreen: the impossibility of finding a fitting body to develop from and into from a mother whose own body was unstable and disregarded. Doreen's mother's chaotic body had, of course, been internalized as the basis of Doreen's own body. This internalized, unstable body could not provide much sense of body security and, coupled with the lack of attention she received from her mother *vis-à-vis* her body, Doreen was unable to inhabit a body she could just live in. The stillness which she found with her father in that late night, quasi somnolent state was crucial in her being able to feel in any continuity in the way of physical identity. But father's stillness wasn't enough.[1] She was always trying, always attending to this ill-fitting home.

How we develop a self

Scholarship within psychoanalysis and attachment theory has focused on the problematic nature of self (Bowlby, 1969; Fairbairn, 1953; Winnicott, 1974, 1979). We know that it is the emotional relationship between baby and mother or primary carers that provides the sustenance, the psychic nourishment for the infant's development of a sense of self. Two conditions are essential for the development of self in the infant. The carer needs to see the baby as separate, as a "being" with its own needs and desires and also needs to see and accept the baby's dependency. In other words, for the baby to feel that what emerges from inside of her or him is okay and thus feel that it exists in an alive way for itself, it needs recognition from another, an intimate and consistent other. Its coos, its initiatives, its cries, its curiosities, need to be acknowledged, seen, and responded to. Repeated experiences of recognition is the way the baby comes to have a sense of self as generative and vibrant. The relational interchange is the emotional food which the baby internalizes in the development of self.

Experiences in which the baby's gestures are consistently misunderstood or interpreted as being about something else, create in the baby a sense that what it produces, its essential productions or me-ness, are somehow wrong, and then the baby's sense of self has to develop to incorporate this painful and confusing psychological reality.

There are several ways we conceptualize the developing psyche managing this psychic reality. In the first instance, Fairbairn argues, the psyche "blames" itself. When hurt, harmed, ignored, the baby renders its helplessness as a form of power. It imagines what it could do to change the situation. It is not in a position to blame the mother or carers for that would make it feel too powerless and endangered. Instead it inverts its own powerlessness, taking all responsibility for its inability to get the recognition it requires. We recognize such operations well from our clinical work when we are with a patient who thinks the solution to emotional difficulty is to change this or that about themselves, who second-guesses their behaviours in an "if only I had . . .", which in all its manifestations involves the preservation of the desired other as infallible. A Winnicottian statement of this position might be that when a baby's own gestures are repeatedly ignored or remain unreflected on, it finds the part of itself or develops those aspects of self that the mothering person can receive. It looks for confirmation of self through bringing forth attributes, activities, and emotions acceptable and pleasing to its primary care-giver. It takes on and finds within itself the gestures of its mother as a means of holding her within the relationship (Winnicott, 1979).

In a general sense, of course, this is what we all do; we make relationships based on the shared recognition of various aspects of self. The problem arises when the self we present or inhabit is a self that is so reliant on another's recognition that the self *as self* feels fraudulent, not reliable, is labile and needs to be constantly confirmed in order to feel its existence.

How we develop a body

Everything I have just said also applies to the body. The body that is not received, the body that has no body to meet in its development becomes a body that is as precarious, fractured, defended, and unstable as a precarious psyche. Like Winnicott's false self (which is perhaps better thought of as an adapted self), this adapted precarious body not only requires constant affirmation but is so lacking in continuity that its viability for the individual is in question. As Winnicott would argue in relation to the psyche, so too the precarious body, which also depends upon creating and surviving emergencies. Through being thwarted, through having to create itself anew all the time the precarious body gathers a kind of strength from recovering from emergencies. This surviving of or recovering from emergencies provides the individual with the sense that their body exists. And I think we can see this clearly with Rob and with Doreen. In their daily or hourly emergency bodies they show us about their early intersubjective body relationship, the crisis-ridden nature of them and their subsequent search via that same idiom to find the body affirmation they never received.

The body, then, is not a thing in and of itself, not even the integral or material basis of an individual's life, but the body, like the psyche, has relational and object relational elements to it. The body is only made in relationship. It doesn't exist in any viable way outside of relationship, and the body of the baby is introduced to the specific ways of being human through a parental, usually a maternal, relationship, which encodes the ideas and the idioms ascribed to the body in that particular culture.

In contrast, and to make the point more starkly, children who have raised themselves in the wild do not have bodies that move or gesticulate in ways that we would readily identify as human. They take on the attributes of the animals that the child has grown alongside. Wild children do not masturbate and are not sexual in ways that we would recognize. They do not necessarily move about on two legs all the time and they do not develop speech (Lane, 1978).

Everything about our human gesture, about how we move, how we are held, how we experience the arms of carers, our experience of their skin and our skin with their skin, the quality of the touch with which they hold us, the physical reassurance, the soothing, the rocking, the swaddling, which is absorbed at a physical level and becomes our physical mimetic. Similarly, the misreading of our physicality in gruff or inappropriate touch, physical neglect, or physical punishment or punitive regimens—think of the Schreber case—provides our fundamental body sense. If our feeding needs are responded to with just the right amounts and with just the right flow for us, and if we can experience the feeding relationship as mutually satisfying, not only will we have physical confidence where appetite is concerned but we imbibe the idea that other appetites that arise within us will similarly be responded to with pleasure. We are not frightened of ourselves and we are not frightened of our bodily selves. Our raw physicality received with interest and delight becomes the material from which we make our body sense and from which our confidence can flow.

To paraphrase Winnicott's famous and oft-repeated phrase, "there is no such thing as a baby", there is also, I suggest, *no such thing as a body, there is only a body in relationship with another body.*

The body of the developing baby comes from the body of her or his mother, both literally and in terms of the psychic history which bequeaths her relation to that body.[2] The social rules around bodies,

around sexuality, around what kind of body one can have and be in are initiated in the intimate bodily exchanges between carers and babies. How a mother sees a baby's body, whether she perceives it as beautiful or "good", or cute, just like her first child's body, or awful and greedy like her own body, or inconsolably discontent or graceless, is a crucial feature of the transformation of the way in which organs, cells, muscles, bones, tone, smile, transmute into body sense.

To make clear how crucial the early relationship is on a baby's subjective sense of its own body, we can look at gender, perhaps the most social of all constructs, and see how gender has to be written onto the biology of the baby. Girls do not just become girls and boys just become boys. This is an outcome of relationship, fantasy, projection, role expectation, prescription, and culture enforcement. Our perception of the baby's gender is part of the imaginal body we bring to the baby. (when we have a different perception, as in Stoller's cases (Stoller, 1968), the gender identity of the child is confused and unstable). The body we can see for the baby, the body we can imagine for the baby, joins together with the body that we bring to the baby ourselves as the baby makes its own subjective sense of its own body.

The work of Trevarthen (2003) shows delight reflected and reflected. But we know that because of the breeding of body insecurity in women over the last fifty years many women are tragically uneasy as regards their bodies. They cannot take their bodies for granted. They do not live from them. They are not sure of them. Their unconscious solution is to treat their own bodies as emergencies. By food manipulation, bouts of intense exercise, dieting, purging, and cutting, they are always creating and recovering from an emergency in the Winnicottian sense. This provides a sense of continuity where none would otherwise exist.

These crisis-laden, needing recognition bodies are the bodies and the body ambience that women bring to their baby girls, in particular, who then, in my clinical experience, grow up to be women with a great instability in their bodies. Some mothers with this difficulty are able to see their boys' bodies as different and not subject to the same troubled projections but, as we saw, this was not so with Rob, who acutely felt the absence of a body from which to develop. Of course fathers and the paternal body are not absent from our body identity, as I think Doreen's circumstances show us. In fact, for many women, as I have earlier suggested (Orbach, 1999), the father's benign still lap is a physical experience of considerable positive significance as much as the negative significance of a father's fear of a daughter's pubescent body.

I hope you will understand that in drawing attention to the relational nature of the body and the mother's role in the child's experience of her or his body, I am not wishing to criticize mothers. Mothers today have been subject to the most massive onslaught and attack on their bodies. This attack has come from those industries breeding body insecurity (Orbach, 1986), which has intensified the kind of foreboding women have always carried in relation to their bodies in which femininity, particularly female sexuality, has been represented as being extremely dangerous and in need of containment and denial, usually in the form of maternality (Orbach, 1978).

The body of the patient

The question of the body is important because at present, by mentalizing physical experiences, we are missing crucial dimensions in our patients' experience. We are perpetuating a kind of hyper-psychism, if I can call it that. Developing the cerebral capacities of our patients at the expense of understanding their physical development. If we focus on their physical development via the body counter-transference we learn many interesting things that enhance our work.

Body difficulties come in many different guises. Some people experience their bodies in a paradoxical sense as a void, not really knowing how it is plotted, where it begins and ends. Other people experience their body as a hated attribute; for others, it means having this thing, the body, which is out of control. For others it is always just an elusive size away from providing contentment. For still others, they take their own bodies as their object. Such difficulties, from the extreme to what we now take as ordinary discontent, can then lead the individual to become involved in a kind of physical obsession with self in the attempt *to create a body object that didn't exist from the beginning. They try to fill the void by creating a body for themselves. By doing to, touching, picking at, criticizing, fretting, cutting, fussing, manipulating, abusing, caring, and obsessing in one way or another over this body, they concretize for themselves something that has not felt alive.* These are not simply obsessive activities. That is to miss the serious nature of the *search for a body.*

If we bring the body into the therapeutic relationship, which is what I believe many of my patients are asking for, we then have a chance to recognize the missing bodies and reverse the ravages of body hatred. Instead of avoiding the body difficulties we address them. This is a complex and poignant process. We must first welcome the hated body or the disintegrated-in-bits body, the body that is a void, the precarious adapted body, the body that can only weep, scratch, or scream. It is from this standpoint that we we can help our patients build from what is and what was rather than fictionalizing their experience of hated bodies (Orbach, 1993, 1995).

Unwittingly, when faced with the horror many people in therapy feel about or towards their bodies, we can be tempted to not quite hear the pain, even when our interventions sound impeccable. We may find ourselves offering what can only amount to false assurance rather than grappling with the patient's distress. What is required, however, is to find a way not to be frightened of the hate or the disintegrated or voided bodies of our patients so that we can address their pain. We know that pain diminishes or disperses when it has been addressed not sweet-talked.

The body of the psychotherapist

The second thing I believe we need to be able to do is to bring our own bodies to the therapeutic encounter: to not leave them out of the relationship. Our patients are already using our bodies just as they use our psyches. The issue is how we can help them use them actively, consciously, and effectively.

Many people working as therapists find the confrontation with one's own body particularly challenging. It can be extremely discomforting to recognize that our bodies are being scrutinized by our patients not just for how we look but for how we are in them, whether we project comfort and ease, whether we change size, and whether we feel safe enough to let our patients use our bodies as we encourage them to use our psyches. It is obvious, once we reflect upon it, that our patients will be wanting and needing our bodies to be in the room as something that they can work with in the therapy. If therapy is an intersubjective experience, this must surely include our bodies too.

So what does this mean? Does it mean we have no place to hide as our patients see and sense everything? (Others of course see nothing and that is another kind of problem.) In a sense we *are* personally exposed, of course. But having nowhere to hide is one of the wonderful opportunities that working psychotherapeutically offers us as therapists. We get the chance, and are required, to be reflecting upon our own processes. Our reflections help us tremendously. They allow us to shift our relation to ourselves, to expand our emotional repertoires, to enter more fully into our own sensibilities. The counter-transference and our awareness of it is something we can treasure and embrace because of the amazing openings it give us personally as well as in our work. But of course it doesn't just happen. We have to pay attention. We have to look, listen, feel, and interrogate ourselves. And if we pay the same kind of attention to our body nuances and body feelings as we do to our more commonly apprehended counter-transference, I think we will have a great deal to offer those with troubled bodies and body symptoms.

I want to say in closing that we are at an exciting moment in looking at a very neglected area. By looking at it, we skew the picture, because, of course, it is very hard to separate mind and body. But we do need to try to do this in order not to rebalance the tilt towards a rather too cerebral turn within psychoanalysis. So little has been mapped out for us and so little thought about. A lot of our endeavours will have to be provisional but I don't think that should stop us staking a claim for this territory. At a clinical level it has been of enormous value to the people I work with that the body can be addressed in its own terms rather than solely for what it symbolizes. It has given them a way into bodies that often felt chaotic, dangerous, disorganized; that have only made their presence felt through pain, illness, and anxiety. Focusing on the body has helped them find a home which is both psychic and corporeal, and has helped me to realize that the body's development is every bit as crucial as the mind's. Work in this area points strongly towards the need to retheorize the relationship between body and mind and its impact on practice.

Thank you.

Notes

1. It was a version of the still lap of the father which has provided a balm against the activity/neglect spectrum of the maternal relation to the baby girl's body (Orbach, 1999).
2. Of course women also give boys their bodies, which raises very interesting questions about the nature of otherness, of gender, of both female and male sexuality, and the role of the mother in the development, acceptance, and integration of that sexuality.

References

Aron, L., & Anderson, F. S. (Eds.) (1998). *Relational Perspectives on the Body*. Hillside, NJ: The Analytic Press.

Bowlby, J. (1969). *Attachment, Vol. I Attachment and Loss*. London: Hogarth Press.

Brunet, O., & Lezine, I. (1966). *I Primi Anni del Bambino*. Rome: Armando.

Carrol, L. (1865). *Alice in Wonderland*. London: Macmillan.

Chodorow, N. (1978). *The Reproduction of Mothering*. Berkley, CA: University of California Press.

Eichenbaum, L., & Orbach, S. (1982). *Understanding Women*. Harmondsworth: Penguin.

Eichenbaum, L., & Orbach, S. (1983). *What Do Women Want?* London: Michael Joseph.

Farbairn, W. R. D. (1953). *Psychoanalytic Studies of the Personality*. London: Tavistock.

Lane, H. (1978). *The Wild Boy of Aveyron*. Boston, MA: Harvard University Press.

McDougall, J. (1989). *Theatres of the Body; A Psychoanalytic Approach to Psychosomatic Illness*. London: Free Association Books.

Orbach, S. (1978). *Fat is a Feminist Issue*. London: Paddington Press.

Orbach, S. (1982). *Fat is a Feminist Issue II*. London: Paddington Press.

Orbach, S. (1986). *Hunger Strike*. London: Faber and Faber.

Orbach, S. (1994). Working with the false body. In: A. Erskine & D. Judd (Eds.), *The Imaginative Body* (pp. 1676–179). London: Whurr.

Orbach, S. (1995). Counter-transference and the false body. In: *Winnicott Studies 10* (pp. 3–13). London: Karnac.

Orbach, S. (1999). *The Impossibility of Sex.* Harmondsworth: Allen Lane.

Sinason, V. (Ed.) (2002). *Attachment, Trauma and Multiplicity: Working with Dissociative Identity Disorder.* London: Brunner-Routledge.

Stoller, R. (1968). *Sex and Gender.* London: Hogarth Press.

Trevarthen, C. (2003). *Video of Babies.* John Bowlby Memorial Conference, London, 7 March 2003.

Winnicott, D. W. (1971). *Playing and Reality.* London: Tavistock.

Winnicott, D. W. (1965). *The Maturational Process and the Facilitating Environment.* London: Hogarth Press.

Winnicott, D. W. (1975). *Through Paediatrics to Psychoanalysis.* London: Hogarth Press.

The John Bowlby Memorial Lecture 2003

The body in clinical practice

Part Two
When touch comes to therapy

Susie Orbach

> "That's my squeeze machine . . . some people call it my hug machine. . . . it exerts a firm but comfortable pressure on the body, from the shoulder to the knees."
>
> As she lies in her machine . . . she feels that the machine opens a door into an otherwise closed emotional world and allows her, almost teaches her, to feel empathy for others.
>
> Oliver Sacks, *An Anthropologist on Mars* (1995, pp. 263, 264)

Psychoanalysis's discomfort with touch

Sometimes psychoanalysis comes to the ordinary common sense embarrassingly late. Tell someone not in the field that touch is crucial to human psychological and physical development and you'd get a contemptuous "daa" and yet we within the non body, and particularly within the psychoanalytic wing, get singularly jittery and uneasy when touch comes to therapy. This can be the case even for those therapists who were trained in body therapies but whose current interests have led them to psychoanalysis. Indeed, so uneasy are we about this that we are either fuzzy and don't think about it or we have a set of rules around no touching as though that could resolve the issue. If we fall into the latter category, patients who touch us can become designated as rule-breakers and their wish to touch us or be touched by us can be interpreted callously as though their or our impulse were dreadfully wrong, pathological, boundary violating. By categorizing them in this way, we avoid engaging with what touch might be about. We move away from psychoanalysis's dictum to welcome and explore the meaning of things. Rather, we can become threatened and deny ourselves access to crucial aspects of individual idiom, desire, and need.

With a few exceptions, we psychoanalytic clinicians leave the discourse and theorizing about touch to the body-orientated therapists and we keep quiet about those hugs, the touch on the shoulder, the hand that needs holding, the kiss that got planted on us. In so doing we short-circuit an attempt to think about when and why we should or shouldn't touch. What are our and our patients' needs, desires, fears of, and confusions re touch? Unlike other psychoanalytic activities, touch is just off limits.

When something becomes off limits without being much thought about or, rather, thought about anew from time to time, we are in danger of fossilizing. Our field, our collective and individual practice, diminishes. I am very mindful that this is the Bowlby Memorial Lecture. For me, it is very much in the pioneering spirit of John Bowlby if I say at this point that I myself am not sure of exactly how I feel about touch. I believe that Bowlby himself was not exactly sure what he thought about early childhood attachment when he set out to see if he could understand for himself what was really going on in the early mother–baby relationship. Bowlby's project demonstrated the absolute centrality of understanding real attachments in order to understand the human inner world. Attachment theory is the epidemiology of modern psychotherapy and has given us the working paradigm for all relational approaches to psychoanalysis. And, as Sir Richard Bowlby has often said at these memorial lectures, his father would be the first to admit that he had just begun the exploration of the significance of human attachment. It is now up to us to explore in as open a manner as possible the vexed issue of touch within psychoanalysis.

Reading the psychoanalytic literature, it is interesting to see how this issue attempts to assert itself and then gets lost. There are review papers about every twenty years,[1] there are attempts to theorize touching therapy and psychoanalysis, but they don't really develop or, at least, I don't know about those developments, or they have the same problem I was discussing in Part 1 of this lecture, they are about the body and touch as containing *the deepest truth* about the psyche or how purposeful touch in therapy—a hand on an abdomen for example—can provide relief via tears or a slowing down in breathing rather than about the body and touch warranting attention in its own right. That said, I have every expectation that after our conference conversations we shall all have advanced our understanding of the role of touch in the therapeutic encounter. I know I will be further along than my personal ruminations can take me.

How can we think about benign touch?

We therapists know how absolutely critical benign and loving touch is in both early development and in life in general. We enter our first love affair with life viscerally, either vaginally or via a Caesarean, and through skin to skin, mouth to nipple, face on breast, enclosed by arms we start our journey. We enter human culture through a relationship in which we require touch and we need to touch others. Touch is the bio-psychic means by which we feel our bodies and the bodies of others. Touch initiates our subjective bodily sense.[2]

What psychoanalytic therapists don't know is about benign, thoughtful touch in therapy. To be fair to us, we know a good deal about malign touch by therapists. We know about the disaster that is sexual aggression by therapists. We know about the kind of invasive and inaccurate interpreting which reaches in and with a searing touch fractures an individual's fragile sense of self.

What we haven't focused on and haven't theorized about are why we might touch, why we might not touch, what's going on inside of us when we think about being touched or touching, what the interpersonal intra-psychic pressures may be that mean we feel impelled to do so. Nor, because we don't talk about it, have we approached what happens in the therapy relationship, within the transference when a benign touch is offered but experienced as disturbing. Or what a patient makes of a body language that clearly indicates that our invitation to explore everything does not really mean everything because touch is *verboten*. Nor do we even know what a person we work with might make of our physical closedness, our reticence, or refusal to hug. Nor, because of the taboo on touch, do we discuss among ourselves what we can make of stepping forward into the patient's space as though to hug them before a long break, for example, and discovering we've done the wrong thing. We don't discuss it because we don't do it or rather we don't admit to doing it. Thus we have little data to discuss with one another in the psychoanalytic world about touch.

We have one highly discussed case in which Patrick Casement (1985) discloses changing his mind about holding the hand of his patient as she relives the trauma of her mother's letting her hand go when she was being operated on as a child. In *On Learning from the Patient* Casement tells us that he withdraws his offer to hold her hand lest he fixate his patient rather than enable her to relive the trauma and come through it. In his earlier and recent discussions of this case (Casement, 2002) and his decision not to touch, he is aware that he re-enacts through his own withdrawal the mother's withdrawal. He recognizes that he precipitates a breakdown through not touching and in his latest appraisal of the case he argues that acceding to her request to touch would have been easy. The hard part was *not* touching.

Although I find Casement's argument convincing for him, what it seems to leave out is the understanding of the desire for touch as being co-created between analyst and analysand. We have an account in which the patient is the person who registers on Casement, who is, as it were, almost an outsider rather than that the analyst is someone who, by his previous actions with the patient, made possible or conveyed the possibility, the idea, that holding was needed and that touch could happen. Without wanting to take away from Casement's thoughtfulness and evident concern for the patient, I am left with a sense (more so in his later rather than his first discussion) that Casement sees the patient as the only actor on the therapeutic stage and Casement's response then as being entirely reactive rather than the outcome of an intersubjective, interpersonal, and idiosyncratic exchange.

Touch and attachment

But perhaps a more challenging theoretical point for me relates to two areas. One is the continual dismissal by psychoanalysis of the materiality of the body which might question whether this woman could have her body, a body which had been burnt, soothed entirely through words. The second is about another dismissal: the bypassing or disregard of the work on the bio-psychological significance of touch, both in development and in everyday life.

In 1947 Renee Spitz reported on hospitalism (Spitz, 1960). He reported that those babies in the hospital ward given the same feeding and changing but who were closest to the nurses' station and who received a few more touches as the nurses passed by them more frequently, survived, while those furthest away failed to thrive. This has been an important psychoanalytic finding that we have somehow stripped of its physicality as we have taken it with us into practice. We've interpreted Spitz's finding as to do with the centrality of relationship: the baby needs to be held in mind, the baby needs contact, but like so many of the things we were discussing, the touch part, the physical interaction, the body to body contact, has somehow become lost in the discussion during this post Second World War mentalist period of psychoanalysis. It is as though we have to learn again what was being written and observed and we have to draw on other fields because we've lost the eye to see what is in front of us in our neglect of this area.

Harlow's monkeys, who craved touch and attached themselves to wire monkeys covered with terry cloth but without a bottle in preference to wire monkeys with a bottle, was another conclusive bit of evidence about the critical function of physical feel and touch in attachment. But again these bits of evidence were not, *are* not evaluated by psychoanalysis for the clinical significance of touch, but for the significance of attachment behaviour as though attachment were a purely mental construct. My experience with patients' attempts to create a body in some of the ways I discussed earlier is in essence a response to touch hunger. It is not just a tautology to rename material as such. Without going into the neurobiology of touch (Field, 1990), it is surely irresponsible to ignore the findings of the Miami Touch Research Institute, which show that "a hand on a shoulder" can reduce the heart rate and lower the blood pressure, or Vivette Glover's work on oxytocin, the bonding hormone, which is increased through loving touch and which creates a sense of bio-psychological well-being. (Glover, 2001). Touch can be healing, and although it is unfashionable to say so, psychoanalysis is also very much about healing, and I wonder what kind of disservice we do by *not* touching.

Touch is a fundamental way in which we come into our subjective sense of our body. The psyche somatic unity which Winnicott talks of as being crucial to the sense of an aliveness is less a magical process that either goes right or goes wrong and is more one we need to and are beginning to understand. Touch is one of the ways, the physical vehicles (if I can be so mechanical about a sense) through which the maternal body manifests its connection to the potential other and the body other that is the baby. Without physical touch, the baby cannot flourish. The kind of touch and touching the baby receives structures their subjective relation to her or his body and makes possible or problematic, and all the states in between those two poles, the sense of aliveness of vitality and indwelling, to use another of Winnicott's notions (Winnicott, 1971), that is either taken for granted or repetitively sought.

The preoccupation with the surface of the body, especially the surface as represented through graphic design or photography of either the still or moving variety and its capacity to destabilize the body sense or potential body sense of literally millions of girls and women, works its terrible mischief, in part, because an interior sense of vitality and aliveness has failed to be established. The missing piece is the reticence, the awkwardness, the interruption, and by interruption I mean the cyclical interruption of the impulse to touch. Touch, once absent, tentative, gawky, or inconsistent, fails at both a neural and a psychological level to animate the body for the individual. The touch we are able to give, the touch we respond to, the delight and appreciation of another's physicality, is part of what vivifies a body. Without it, we are in the territory of body as surface, body as symbol, body not as lived experience, but body as text on which we inscribe the desperateness of not having an alive body but only a facsimile body.

And it is psychoanalysis's participation, emphasis, and elevation of the facsimile body, the body as text, the body as drive that must be tamed, that we are trying to rethink at this Bowlby

Memorial Lecture. We have to be courageous enough to invite physicality into the consulting room in more than its symbolic forms. We can comprehend the historical injunctions against touch in a schema that sees the body as the fundamental source of drives and the ways in which sexual drives become converted into hysterias as attempts at drive regulation, but for the taboo on touch to be a passenger to contemporary psychoanalytic theory with its focus on affects, attachment, internal object relations, the struggle for connection and differentiation seems woefully unthought through.

The architecture of the analytic session

One thing that I think our current preoccupations suggests is that the seating position of analyst and analysand, client and therapist, in which the therapist sits to the side of or behind the supine patient, is clearly up for reconsideration. The architecture of bodies in a room and bodies in relation or the difficulties that patients and therapists can experience with embodiment, would seem to militate against the therapist sitting behind the patient. The receiving ear—the main analytic instrument—is both a psychological and a physical receiver. We register and mimetically respond to resonance, timbre, tone, interruption, rapid speech, hesitancy, tears, speechlessness. But we register and respond as though in doing so we are actually responding to the physicality of the person rather than as we are doing, responding to a representation or a truncated version of their issues around physicality, embodiment, corporeality. The metaphors we grab for in describing the couch as holding or containing are words denoting something physical, again as though physicality can be represented by sounds and speech. My clinical experience working face to face suggests that physicality, and the problematic around the patient's physicality is insufficiently addressed as long as we remain in the realm of the symbolic. Symbols are useful for symbolizing but the body, struggling to come alive, struggling to be held, may well need more than symbols. It needs to be engaged with, struggled with, to feel welcomed, put upon, invaded, affronted, moved, turned on, and turned off by a body in the room. Without a body to see, without a body experience in the room, we psychoanalytic types can reprise an elaborate confirmation of disembodiment and prohibition in which defensiveness and false or dead bodies reign supreme.

Of course, against this you might argue that speech—words— like feelings are a physical activity. Words are not a mentalist practice. Language is the enunciation of our psyche somatic nature. Words can reach us very deeply—and when we say deeply, we mean they can move us, and when we say they can move us we mean we feel something shift and change and find a new place. However, despite the physicality of the words we use and the motion we associate with their power, sometimes words are insufficient.

When touch came to therapy

Let's take a couple of cases where something else, touch, came to therapy to see if we can get further. Lest you think I am a touch propagandist or promoting touch in the consulting room, I'm not. I am as uneasy as the next person about raising the issue lest it be misconstrued. I am absolutely not saying let's all touch; let's abandon the taboo. *I am* saying in the context of touch and attachment, let's think about it and see where we get to. This is a question addressed to body psychotherapists as much as to those of us from psychoanalysis. Let's increase our understanding of why we feel moved to do so and why we don't. We don't need to act precipitously. That's not what I am arguing.

And, of course, touch is a personal idiom. Some of us are very prone to touch and be touched. Others of us get "touchy" if we are. And I've pondered on this word. Why "touchy" when we mean very sensitive, irritable, peevish, grouchy, cross, emotionally prickly? Why "touchy" when we mean daring, risky, chancey? Does our language know more than we acknowledge as analytic clinicians about the deficits of not being adequately touched and the consequence then of becoming insufficiently emotionally resilient?

I want to give three brief vignettes. One is a case of a supervisee I've discussed before (Orbach, 1995), of a woman of fifty, Sara, suffering with vaginismus, who requested a hug from her therapist. The therapist, a man, was surprised to discover that he was rather stunned by his response to her request. Her asking for a hug made him recognize his reluctance and catalysed for him something more than discomfort. It made him aware that, uncharacteristically, he was actually quite out of physical sympathy with her. For several sessions around the hug incident, he had experienced a putrid smell in the room like that of a rotting mango. In discussing how he might handle this powerful olfactory counter-transference, he had found a way to see this smell is an expression of her ripeness for the sexual intercourse she longed for. But it is the hug that I wish to focus on now, because it seems to me such a very clear example of a relational communication, in which his wariness or discomfort about receiving or giving her a hug was made possible by her creativity in communicating to him via the counter-transference just how ghastly she felt in her body, how turned off she was to entering into her own body, let alone letting another enter what felt so physically repulsive and unseemly to her.

The hug was absolutely pivotal. In the therapist struggling with his counter-transference so that he could authentically receive the "putrid" body, Sara was able to reverse the corporeal hatred that had stemmed from the touch neglect of her parents, for whom physicality was only medicalized. Her vaginismus dissolved. *Her body, not her symptom, now came to therapy.* It was not a body only closed, or a body only in pain, or a body over ripe, but a body beginning to be accepted. A body on its way to vitality. A body which could receive.

Sara became very excited. She took this new potential body subjectivity and the fact of her not knowing her body in this emerging way as a serious project. She enthusiastically changed the way she dressed, began to decorate the surface because she wanted to adjust and portray the aliveness she newly felt within. Her experiments with style concretized her growing physical fluidity. More impressively still, she could mourn the body she never had, the missed undeveloped body of so many years, the missed body of adolescence and her twenties and thirties and enter into the challenges of the middle-aged body, suddenly awoken.

The physical exchange was, I repeat, pivotal. This woman could not progress delimited by words. She needed a body to accept her body. She needed to hug and be hugged. She needed to feel the welcome when she herself was more than hesitant about her own capacity to accept her new corporeality.

A woman I was seeing adopted her baby, who came to her at six months and was rigid. The baby's legs were stuck straight out ahead of her, whether from fright or trauma, I did not and do not know. The clinical point is that the disruption of the *impulse* to touch enraged this adopting mother. She was shocked to find herself wanting to hurt this baby, to shake it out of its rigid stance. She experienced her daughter's rigidity as both a belligerent affront and as an aggressive passivity. She could not always recognize this six-month-old as a baby, as babies are soft. Her baby's physicality became inscrutable, challenging her with its immobility.

In the therapy, we had to find a way for her to overcome her impulse to hit. I myself wanted to soothe this mother's body. It was as though it was inflamed, and she had become infected by her baby's inability to tolerate touch. But I knew that I couldn't just touch her. That touch would have been too invasive, too much me as the one who could touch in a calming way and she as the one whose touch was only aggression.

One day she brought the baby to a session. She wanted to show me how awful it was for her. I saw what she meant but of course the rigidity did not carry the affronting feelings for me and I felt able to stroke the baby gently, which she received. In the course of the session, my patient began to be able to stroke the baby too. We found a synergistic, gentle rhythm which suited all three of us. I relinquished touching the baby and found that I had begun stroking her arm as though my touch could be a balm to her inflammation. She gained some confidence in touch, first at one remove, and then directly. I had not expected to touch her, in fact I had anticipated quite the opposite, in the event, it seemed the only thing to do. The therapeutic touch reduced her fear, projections, and panic, and in the experience of being soothed released oxytocin—the bonding hormone, which they had both required.

My third and final case is about a hug foisted on me which I did not want or anticipate at the end of a session. In my attempt to surrender to the patient's idiom and receive the hug I pondered what she made of it. I don't feel I am such a successful dissembler that she wouldn't pick up some initial discomfort from me but she didn't seem to for she moved forward towards me to hug me at the end of subsequent sessions. Although I didn't find her hug repulsive, it was definitely unwanted. I didn't feel it was right for me.

I couldn't find a way to bring this up or make sense of it for a considerable time so I bore the hugging when it occurred and hoped I might understand this physical disjuncture. It is not that I haven't been hugged or indeed hugged before. I have. It is my response and its possible meanings that intrigued me.

Jane was involved in a rather cold and cruel relationship with an ex-junkie. It was as though there was a deadness at the heart of him and he couldn't tolerate the warmth that she brought to the relationship, much as he craved it. There was a great deal of push–pull (Eichenbaum & Orbach, 1983) in the relationship and for her some ravaging severings which disturbed her. As she described her experience it seemed to me that dead was absolutely the right word for the chill at the centre of this man, or rather the freeze that occurred when they got close.

Jane talked about her sexual life with him and let slip, and I say let slip because I think she was uneasy about this, that their sex life now involved S&M practices. She saw herself as sexually very free, which interested me given my sense of her body being so unplotted on the one hand and so full of self-disgust on the other. But I took what she said, for what else could I do, and I was intrigued by the turn in the sexual relationship and her discomfort with it. The unsolicited hug began to make sense to me. It was a misreading of the physical exchange between us: a possible parallel process to that which was occurring in the current sex with the boy-friend. It was a physical adjunct, a concretization of the difficulties she was having with the transgression of what felt right to her sexuality. She passed on to me a discomfort, a discomfort that had been passed on to her.

One final point. And this is an idea I can't quite get but am reaching for, and in the spirit of this being a working conference I'd like to seed it as a potential thought. Touch, or abandoning the taboo on touch within psychoanalysis, seems to me a part of the movement to democratize therapeutic practice. We've moved away from the analyst or therapist as all-knowing to the analyst or therapist being seen and understood as a co-participant in the therapeutic endeavour and specifically a co-creator of the transference–counter-transference ambience and enactment (Mitchell & Aron, 1999). We've come to understand the democratization of the therapy relationship through addressing the paradox of the asymmetries that exist within it. While still privileging the thoughts and feelings of the analysand, we have recognized the central importance of the therapist's thoughts and feelings too, particularly the ones that don't fit, the ones that perplex, the ones we have that seem, on the face of it, counter-therapeutic. In bringing our bodies into the room, we are going a step further in the democratizing of the process. Two bodies, two minds, two souls, two subjectivities.

Does touch, benign, thoughtful, and tender, extend this democracy? Does the touch hunger of the autistic engineer in Oliver Sacks's description at the beginning of this lecture tell us something that is right in front of our eyes? Namely, that reversing touch hunger is a door to empathy for many? Can we find a way for it to or must we remain scared, so scared of its power that we can't contemplate it? And if we can't, what is our theoretical justification—not our rhetoric—that's easy, but our theoretical underpinning to reject it?

Thank you.

Notes

1. See, for example, "On touch in the psychoanalytic situation". *Psychoanalytic Inquiry, 20*(1).
2. I am setting aside a discussion in the new work by Peter Halligan, Antonio Damasio, and V. S.Ramachandran in neurobiology, which is looking at the body from a different perspective and which I think will in time yield extremely interesting results for psychotherapists.

References

Casement, P. (1985). *On Learning from the Patient*. London: Tavistock.
Casement, P. (2002). *Learning from our Mistakes*. Hove, East Sussex: Brunner Routledge.
Eichenbaum, L., & Orbach. S. (1983). *What Do Women Want?* London: Michael Joseph.
Field, T. (1990). *Infancy*. Cambridge MA: Harvard University Press.
Glover, V., Giatu, R., & Fisk, N. M. (2001). Maternal stress in pregnancy and its effect on the human foetus: an overview of research findings. *Stress 4*: 19–203.

Mitchell, S. A., & Aron, L. (Eds.) (1999). *Relational Psychoanalysis: The Emergence of a Tradition*. Hillsdale, NJ: Analytic Press.

Orbach, S. (1995). Countertransference and the false body. *Winnicott Studies* No 10. London: Karnac Books.

Sacks, O. (1995). *An Anthropologist on Mars*. London: Picador.

Spitz, R. (1960). *The First Year of Life*. Madison, CT: International Universities Press.

Winnicott, D. W. (1971). *Playing and Reality*. London: Tavistock.

Touch and the impact of trauma in therapeutic relationships with adults

Anne Aiyegbusi

Introduction

I n my work with highly traumatized women offenders in high security psychiatric hospitals, lack of any experience of loving touch early in life occupies a prominent part of the therapeutic agenda. The impact of emotional deprivation and neglect on the personalities of the patients concerned is intertwined with the impact of emotional, physical, and sexual abuse, making for a complex clinical picture.

In keeping with Fonagy's (1998) theory, the experience of hateful early contact may have been impossible to process mentally. Instead, in adult life, an unpleasant bodily reaction is experienced. Likewise, the need to inflict pain on others as a way of dealing with internal distress can be seen in the women's offending behaviour as well as in their interpersonal relating, where painful communication tends to take place through the counter-transference.

In this paper, I will describe the way in which the patients use their bodies to communicate what cannot be spoken about and in many cases thought about. Additionally, I will describe what it is like to be on the receiving end of powerful counter-transference material and the way interpersonal work can result in physical pain and discomfort.

The case material that I will use throughout this paper is not based on any individual patient or any particular service. It is an amalgam of many experiences of patients and services during ten years of working with traumatized women offenders in high security psychiatric hospitals.

Background

Recent policy developments mean that the way secure care for women is provided will change within the next 2–3 years (Department of Health, 2002, 2003). One outcome is that women are moving relatively rapidly out of the high security hospitals. An implication is that any over-reliance upon the fabric of these closed institutions to contain highly distressed and disturbed behaviour on the part of women patients will cease. Instead, therapeutically robust programmes within less physically secure environments will need to meet the needs of a clinically complex population of women. Therefore, as nurse consultant, my primary task is to develop in the nursing staff skills required to engage more interpersonally with the women patients than may have happened in the past. As such, some of what I am going to talk about reflects my work with nurses, and their work with patients, as well as my work as a therapist.

The women

Women in high security psychiatric hospitals may have been convicted of serious offences, or they may have been convicted of no criminal offence. Either way, it is usually their behaviour on a day to day basis that leads to high security admission and that inevitably includes the emotional impact they have on those whose job it is to provide care, treatment and, in some cases, detention.

Crimes

It is regularly cited that women's offending is less severe than their male counterparts and indeed if the damage done to other people is used as a yardstick, women are less serious offenders. However, as Anna Motz (2001) and Estela Welldon (1988) before her have clarified, women's violence and destructiveness is most likely to be aimed at their own bodies, or those of their children, who are regarded as part of themselves. Anna Motz (2001) uses the term "crimes against the body" to describe the psychosomatic illnesses, bodily acting out such as self injury or eating difficulties and Munchausen's syndrome by proxy behaviour that women offenders bring to the clinical arena. Of course, using the body to commit acts of violence against another person is part and parcel of the picture with regard to forensic patients, both men and women.

Secure attachment experience is a rarity among the population of women detained in high security provision. These were the abandoned babies, the neglected, deprived, abused, and sometimes physically unwell babies who received intrusive medical interventions in the apparent absence of loving touch and close bodily comfort from an available, responsive mother. The most bodily disturbed women tend to be those with the most severe histories of deprivation and abuse. In terms of the physical damage the women patients do to themselves, much of it seems to be understandable in terms of re-enacting past traumatic experience.

Clinical example

Janette is a twenty-five-year-old woman whose self injury is severe. She regularly takes bites out of her own flesh, talking of making herself disappear. She is also a young woman who is very violent to others, particularly carers, who she attacks in the early stages of developing a therapeutic relationship when she is presumably at her most anxious attachment-wise. She perceives tiny slights as betrayal or rejection and often perpetrates severe assaults on these occasions.

Janette was born out of wedlock to a mother who suffered chronic alcoholism and who herself had been adopted as a baby and estranged from her adoptive family for many years. Therefore, there was no apparent support for Janette's mother and no alternative attachment figures available for Janette. Janette required blood transfusions immediately after she was born due to a medical condition. She was later sent home with her mother. At the age of six months, Janette was admitted to the children's hospital with malnutrition, a fractured arm, and evidence of previous injuries. She was placed alternately with her mother and children's homes for a few years. Eventually Janette was fostered into a family who sadly turned out to be abusive to her. Her foster mother was physically abusive and her foster father was physically and sexually abusive. Janette received no love. She was emotionally abused and treated like a slave. She was admitted to the high security hospital at the age of sixteen following a period of violence and damage to property and people. Janette had by this time also been engaged in a long-term, highly destructive relationship with her body, which she could not love, only treat with hatred and contempt.

Counter-transference

As professionals, we come to the workplace with our own traumas, losses, and vulnerabilities, sometimes processed but sometimes unprocessed. Time and again we find that nurses and healthcare assistants who engage with this population of women find themselves disturbed by their work, occasionally to the point of breakdown. It seems that emotional pain is stirred up to the extent that existing defences are no longer effective. The interaction between patients' unprocessed traumatic experience and that experienced by members of staff can amount to a toxic combination. Physical and psychological sickness is then experienced within the staff group. In keeping with traditional psychiatric nursing models, the trend over time has been not to think about what working with the patient group might be stirring up emotionally, and so the danger is that a retreat into illness is experienced as the only solution to unbearable psychic discomfort.

As Richard Davies (1996, p. 133) explains,

> The view is taken that professionals who deal with offenders are not free agents but potential actors who have been assigned roles in the individual offender's own re-enactment of their internal world drama.

The central, unconscious drama of women's secure psychiatric services appears to involve interpersonal abuse and the task of all professionals is to think about this painful material when the pressure is to act out in a sado-masochistic way. Processing such toxic emotional material is extremely difficult, given the potency of experience and since the counter-transference includes humiliation, exposure, rage, and loss, the risk is that instead of processing, professionals act out within the staff group so interactions occur in hurtful ways, including bullying, aggressive practical joking, gallows humour, gossiping, or backbiting. Another way of acting out includes launching envious attacks at colleagues who are getting something good like a course or clinical supervision.

A question frequently asked by nursing staff is "Why does it hurt so much?" People complain a lot about pains in the chest area. I myself went through a stage of fearing that I might have a heart attack at work, for no clear reason other than feeling emotionally overwhelmed by my work over a period of time. I have come to the conclusion that one of the many aspects of human distress that we are invited to process is heartache, which cannot be put to one side. Also, the experience of trauma often involves changes, if not an end to a person's emotional life as it was previously enjoyed, especially that which is the concern of the heart. The same can be the case for professionals who are at risk of becoming vicariously traumatized within services for large numbers of people who have been victimized in the past.

Physical symptoms as care seeking

The long-term consequences for a person who does not feel they have been loved for the person they are, or feels that no interest or value has been paid to their mind or what they think about, may be that the person conceptualizes themselves primarily in terms of their body. When that body appears to be the focus for scrutiny and the only available attention, as is the case in physical and sexual abuse, perhaps the self is even more likely to be conceptualized in physical or bodily terms. This includes using the body to communicate what cannot be spoken or articulated through words. This form of alexithymia accounts for the common currency of expression in women's services. Also, the women may have faith in physical health need as a way to secure input whereas emotional need, if it can be recognized, is not associated with validation or as a means to secure time and responsive input from a carer. In Munchausen's syndrome by proxy, of course, factitious physical health needs are located in a child or other dependent who is then presented for care and treatment. The parent receives some assuagement through the involvement of health care professionals in the child's treatment.

Case example

Wendy baffled the nurses who cared for her. She seemed to explode with rage as if coming from nowhere. However, when nurses began to take account of the way she presented with physical health needs, it was clear that as her distress built up, she increased her complaints. Before lashing out, she was consumed with feelings of being ignored and not cared for and because she sat in a chair smiling, nurses thought she was quite happy. They weren't hearing her complaints because, of course, they were communicated in terms of "aches and pains", "coming down with something", or "needing support for an old injury that was now giving jip". When nurses were helped to link Wendy's physical health communications with her state of mind and to recognize physical health need as a form of care-seeking, an effective programme of care was developed.

Conclusion

Working with a large population of women offenders requires thought about the body, which is constantly brought to the clinical arena. Psychic pain is repeatedly located back into the body where the initial damage was done. Behaviour, language, and the counter-transference tend to focus largely on the body. In this field of work, words can truly hurt and the task of professionals is to process mentally and emotionally that which patients are as yet unable to think about for themselves. In order to do this effectively without secondary retraumatization, staff in turn need appropriate support and clinical supervision for this painful and difficult work.

References

Davies, R. (1996). The inter-disciplinary network and the internal world of the offender. In: C. Cordess & M. Cox (Eds.), *Forensic Psychotherapy: Psychodynamics and the Offender Patient. Part 2. Mainly Practice* (pp. 113–144). London: Jessica Kingsley.

Department of Health (2002). *Women's Mental Health: Into The Mainstream. Strategic Development Of Mental Health Care For Women.* London: HMSO.

Department of Health (2003). *Mainstreaming Gender and Women's Mental Health : Implementation Guidance.* London: HMSO.

Fonagy, P. (1998). An attachment theory approach to treatment of the difficult patient. *Bulletin of The Menninger Clinic, 62*(2): 147–169.

Motz, A. (2001). *The Psychology of Female Violence: Crimes Against the Body.* London: Brunner-Routledge.

Welldon, E. V. (1988). *Mother, Madonna, Whore: The Idealisation and Denigration of Motherhood.* New York: Guilford.

The neurobiology of attachment, touch and the body in early development

Margot Sunderland

Abstract

This presentation focused on the extremely powerful brain and biochemistry activated by touch within the context of an attachment relationship. It addressed how the simple gesture of reaching out, hand to hand, is viewed in many psychotherapeutic circles with such mistrust, the human need for physical comfort and warmth distorted and sexualized. It is argued that the greatest critic is so often the touch-starved child in the adult. He or she has no frame of reference for safe touch, no biochemical childhood experience of safe holding, warm snuggling, or the delight of rough and tumble.

The blight of suspicion and fear of disapproval renders many analysts and psychotherapists silent about their actual practice. They become secret hand holders who only confess to like-minded colleagues. There *is* safe touch in the consulting room, when not to do so would be a failure of compassion. Like all higher mammals, we are genetically programmed to connect through touch, particularly in the case of human beings *in extremis*.

The presentation also addressed what many psychotherapists

are reluctant to face— that there are times when words are not enough, or are just too slow in terms of effecting change. At times touch is far more potent. Too potent?

For child therapy, there are further pressing issues; e.g. the developmental motoric impulse of the child to express their feelings physically. Do we push them off our laps? The fact is that rough and tumble play releases brain fertilizers vital for emotional and social development, and that holding the wild child will establish essential anti-anxiety and anti-rage biochemistry. Does the therapist sidestep this neurobiology because she or he is afraid?

Bowlby Memorial Conference 2003

Body counter-transference: more questions than answers

Compiled by Sarah Benamer and Kate White

There were eighteen small groups convened by experienced members of CAPP to provide an opportunity for discussion and reflection. The aims of these groups were to:

- explore and respond to the examples of body counter-transference given by speakers in earlier sessions and provide space to reflect on responses to what participants have heard so far;
- invite participants to share experiences of touch with their own early carers and how these might have shaped their experiences of their bodies and in this context to discuss the impact of race, gender, disability, class in different cultural settings and their impact on bodily relating in therapeutic relationships;
- think about question/s that the group would like discussed by the panel at the plenary.

It was thought that the group facilitators might wish to encourage participants to explore their own experiences of touch and the body as experienced or envisaged in therapeutic settings—for example, revulsion, disgust, the erotic, sexuality, threat, fear, danger, and love.

The themes and questions that were raised fell into two main groups: touch, and the therapists' counter-transference experiences in relation to the body. Issues of culture and difference were linked into both themes.

Touch

An initial question raised and explored in some groups was about whether the role of the therapist is to give the client experience of a relationship that they have needed and have not had. If so, particularly since in our culture many people are touch deprived, and since loving touch is a primary biological and psychological need, does our role as therapist include the provision of loving physical touch when the client needs it as part of the whole human experience that we offer? Is it the fear of litigation or the fear of our own bodies that stops us from touching?

Are there any ground rules that might inform our decision about whether or not to touch? A further issue explored in the groups was the question of how a therapist who does not touch works with someone who has been touch deprived without repeating the deprivation.

There were a whole group of questions about maintaining safe boundaries, negotiating consent and clarity about who initiates touch—therapist or client. Although touch can be soothing, for example with chaotic children, the dangers of misinterpretation are significant. There may be a need to think through the client's expectations of boundaries. Another concern people wanted the panel to discuss was the potential loss of a reflective space when a therapist actually touches his or her client, and the possibility of foreclosing exploration of the fantasies around touch. Should we disclose our counter-transference in these moments and if so, how?

Touch and themes of difference

Participants considered the impact of gender and whether male and female touch are different. What about aggressive touch? The cultural body and touch? If you *are* touching what are the boundaries and how are they culturally derived? In particular, how might therapists behave with people whose experience of touch has been negative? What is the impact of touch and bodily experience in people from different sexualities when homophobia is so prevalent and hatred of body difference so widely expressed in our culture? Similar questions arose regarding people with disabilities.

Other forms of touch that are not physical

Many groups opened up questions around finding connectedness and intimacy—"being touched"—through words, body language, eye contact, and the sound, musicality, physicality, and rhythm of the voice.

Therapists' body counter-transference experiences

Participants shared their experiences of counter-transference, concluding that ultimately this resonates in the body. There were wide-ranging and vibrant conversations in this component of the discussion, for example:

- Loathing/shame/disgust—what do we do with these feelings? How do we process them? What do we do with this powerful "body stuff" we feel?
- Do we comment on our clients' bodies?
- What is it like for us to have nowhere to hide in the consulting room? How do we respond to personal questions about our bodies; for example, "Do you shave your legs?" What does it *feel* like when a client comments on your body? How do you respond to your body either being appropriated or not seen by the client? Consideration was given to the questions of how, when, and if we might acknowledge physical counter-transference to the client.
- How should we let our bodily selves be used as an instrument in the therapy, particularly if we are women? What do we mean by "instrument"? Are there clients to whom we do not want to surrender our bodies? (However, it was recognized

that in any therapeutic dyad self-regulation and mutual regulation can be seen as akin to the person's early feeding relationships. Thus early bodily-derived relational patterns are likely to be reproduced and need to be recognized and understood in the therapeutic relationship. There was recognition that to do this work we do need to find ways to protect and look after ourselves, bodily and emotionally.)

- How do we keep holding the symbolic and metaphoric and the body? We do not want to swing to the body end of the spectrum in reaction to the question around mentalizing—we want to oscillate between mind and body and be able to hold both.
- What happens to the self when the body breaks down in illness—particularly in ageing? The subtlety of working with elderly people and how the counter-transference can affect the therapist in a dysregulating way was considered by one group in particular.

Other questions which were explored included:

- What about boys' and men's bodies?
- How do we share our vulnerability about sexual issues and the recognition of erotic counter-transference?
- How do we acknowledge and understand more effectively the difference and uniqueness of bodies, including cultural difference?
- What are the training implications of this work on attachment, touch and the body?

In conclusion, it is clear that there was a wide-ranging discussion in the small groups and many people appreciated the opportunity to explore the themes of the conference in a more intimate setting. It also meant that participants had time to reflect upon and think through some of the questions they were then able to raise in the plenary later that day. However, it was also recognized that, since this was a working conference, the discussions and final plenary left us with many more questions than answers. They have provided us with a rich and creative resource for further reflection and exploration.

Sarah Benamer is a psychotherapist in training at CAPP and Kate White is a member of CAPP.

Touch: attachment and the body

A review of CAPP's Tenth Bowlby Memorial
Conference 2003[1]

Morwenna Opie

Touch: attachment and the body, was a theme that emerged from feedback from last year's conference. This fact, and a very distinguished list of speakers, contributed to an extremely successful conference with impressive attendance and enthusiastic delegate involvement. Pia Duran, John Bowlby's daughter, was in attendance, and she commented on her pleasure in seeing how the memorial conference was going from strength to strength. This, I think, is a testament to the continuing importance that attachment research has to contemporary psychological theory and practice, and its relevance to the broad range of clinicians and academics represented at the conference.

Those who braved a wet and cold Friday night to be at the opening evening were extremely well rewarded with a fascinating presentation by Colwyn Trevarthen, Professor (Emeritus) of Child Psychology and Psychobiology at the University of Edinburgh. In his talk, entitled "Intimate contact from birth", Professor Trevarthen used engaging video footage of parent–child interaction to outline the theory of communicative musicality. Highlighting evidence of children's abilities to interact and express emotions, even in the first weeks of life, he suggested that attachment work perhaps underestimated a child's capacities. He explored how aspects of interaction (exploited by, but not exclusive to, music) including pulse, quality, and narrative, enable "coordinated companionship" to emerge. In his conceptualization, there is "more to touch than touch", such that in addition rhythm, voice, and expression are important aspects of attachment bonding.

It was appropriate that on International Women's Day Susie Orbach, acclaimed author of *Fat is a Feminist Issue* and co-founder of the Women's Therapy Centre, gave the John Bowlby Memorial Lecture. She explored the body in clinical practice, including body counter-transference and the significance of touch in the therapeutic encounter. In a provocative and interesting presentation using illuminating case-examples, she referred to the fact that attachment is a very physical theory. She outlined her emerging belief that the body should not be unduly "mentalized" by therapists, but recognized "in and of itself". After outlining experiences of clients who had "bodies searching to become bodies", the second part of her lecture explored the therapist's role in bringing bodies into the therapeutic encounter. She concluded that perhaps abandoning the taboo of touch in a psychoanalytic setting was a necessary part of the democratization of the approach.

Pat Cohen concluded the morning with a brief but illuminating case study, a dramatic example of counter-transference. In doing so she provided a rich and powerful example of work with traumatized individuals. Anne Aiyegbusi, Nurse Consultant at the Women's Service at Broadmoor Hospital, also explored the emotional impact of working with traumatized individuals, in this case nursing staff working with women offenders. In a very sensitive presentation she explored the difficulties facing staff in terms of touching patients, and the need to consider a policy where it was acceptable to touch inmates to search them, but not to comfort in times of distress.

The taboo against touching in the therapeutic encounter was further challenged by Margot Sunderland in an excellent presentation exploring the neurobiology of attachment and the importance of touch. She emphasized that touch is essential for engaging the brain's capacity to release uplifting and "anti-anxiety" chemistry. She suggested that failed therapy should be considered that which does not elicit a change in habitual chemical imbalances. She challenged that if a child who is not comforted when distressed can experience brain damage, should a therapist's fear of touch being perceived as sexualized prevent it taking place? A suggestion that a code of ethics regarding touch should be established with the parents of children seen by therapists was of interest to a great number of the delegates present.

The conference was very provocative, stimulating extensive discussion about the "taboo" of touch and the body in the context of psychoanalytic psychotherapy. Bowlby was, of course, powerfully aware of the child's need for touch and the proximity of the body of the mother, and corresponding traumatic experiences of separation and loss—and his work informed practice, for example in hospital settings. It was, then, appropriate that issues of therapist–client touch were explored at his Memorial Conference. Overall, the conference was a useful and interesting exploration of the complex interwoven themes of touch, attachment, and the body, and their emergence in a therapeutic context.

Note

1. Opie, M. (2003). Bowlby and Attachment. Conference report in The Bridge, The Newsletter of the Association for Child Psychology and Psychiatry, 29: -5 Reprinted with permission of ACPP.

Touch: Attachment and the body
A review of CAPP's Tenth Bowlby Memorial Conference 2003

Sarah Jack

What a stimulating and challenging conference this was! A thought-provoking theme soon emerged, the question of when, where, or how to use touch in the consulting room. This began a weekend of discussions addressing the polarization between psychoanalysis at one end of the continuum and body psychotherapy at the other. I mentally placed attachment-based psychotherapists somewhere in the middle, as I feel we have adopted an approach that assesses individual situations, and that touch has not been assumed to be out of the question. It was pleasing to see that the rigid boundaries that psychoanalysis has adhered to were softening. The question considered was that maybe there are not only some occasions when touch can be extremely powerful for a client, more powerful than the verbal and symbolic exploration of the client's desire for touch, but that for some clients touch might be the only avenue to facilitate a breakthrough.

Susie Orbach highlighted the secrecy and shame therapists feel if they have touched their clients and the shame the client feels if their impulse for physical contact with us is made to feel wrong through our hesitancy or withdrawal. We might be recoiling from touch either through running back to our psychotherapeutic "shoulds and should nots" or, for some reason, we cannot bear the idea of touching them, because we fear being impinged upon, consumed, moved, excited, turned on, or turned off. Susie felt that indeed the client's body needed to be welcomed into the room to feel all of these things. At the same time she sought to give us as therapists permission for our bodies to be experiencing sensations too. Questions were raised as to whether this would open up chasms, as well as concerns that touch would increase the client's dependency needs. Surely the consulting room is the best place for opening chasms and if touch increases a client's dependency needs this can be worked with and through, albeit more demanding for therapists.

Our bodies are inlaid with hundreds of experiences of how we have been handled and held, soothed or intruded upon, touched or neglected, in stillness or in bombardment, and for rougher or smoother. Just as a baby isn't just a baby—it comes with the experiences of being with another—so do our bodies come with the experience of being with another. Susie referred to the body as "elephant", never forgetting its experiences, but unfortunately so ignored. She wanted us to remember that the body is relational and has developed in the context of our social and cultural environment.

With this in mind, Susie was keen to encourage us to bring our bodies into the therapeutic encounter and invited us to consider how we felt about her body and attire, and how we felt about our own bodies in the consulting room. Do we clothe our bodies in a professional uniform, are we too scruffy, too sexy, too brightly clothed, or too drearily dressed? Has our style changed? Does our style change for certain clients? How would we feel if clients were readily to comment? Do we feel we "should" dress in a certain way? Are we keen to hide our bodies or do we remain too scared to bring them into the room? What does this say about our comfort about being ourselves in our own bodies, and how might this hold back a client from using our body in order to develop their own sense of their body?

Margot Sunderland, in delightful picture form, explained how oxytocin and opioids are released in the body by safe and comfortable touch describing how these chemicals allow us to blossom and to feel a sense of satisfaction. Some clients have never had the deep sense of calm and well-being that comes with safe touch and, therefore, have never experienced these anti-anxiety chemicals. Instead, life's accumulation of trauma has flooded a client's body with the dysregulating stress chemicals cortisol and adrenalin, hence the phrase "living off adrenalin". Margot felt that sometimes words were just not able to touch someone in a way that the brain needed in order to experience the release of oxytocin and opiods. However, if a therapy has gone well and a client has been able to experience a safe way of being with another person the cumulative effect of the therapy relationship leads to the reduction of cortisol levels.

Colwyn Trevarthen showed us very memorable video clips of infants communicating with their hands or with sound, in rhythm with their mothers or fathers. His research showed how babies remembered tunes and would join in their mother's singing with the equivalent baby babble vowels. He had noticed that generally mothers used a pitch of middle C, unless they were depressed, when they used lower C. He had observed that when the baby imitates mum, baby's heart rate goes up, and when baby initiates, like a baby babble version of asking a question and waiting for an answer, the baby's heart rate goes down. He had also noticed that during a mother and baby conversation, if the volume of the mother's voice became quieter, the baby would vocalize more loudly, as if to say, "Where are you? Come back!" Colwyn emphasized the rhythm and musicality of the mother and baby's conversations and Susie compared this to the therapist having to get to know and attune to the clients rhythm whilst holding on to their own rhythm. She also commented on the struggle for many women to maintain their own rhythm, as they are so used to getting into the rhythm of others wherever they go and whomever they are with.

Anne Aiyegbusi's presentation provided us with insight into the repetition of abuse which takes place in mentally disordered offenders' units where staff, ill-prepared for the counter-transference, may inadvertently become rejecting and cruel to the patients. Understandably, there was a high proportion of staff who just couldn't cope, disturbed to the point of breakdown, becoming sick or leaving altogether.

Pat Cohen shared a case study of working with a very traumatized woman, which illustrated working with overwhelming counter-transference and her struggle to survive it and remain emotionally able to hold the client.

By the end of a fulfilling weekend, with many thoughts jiggling around in our minds, some questions remained unanswered. In particular the discussion of "how, when, and where" to touch was left very open. I think this was because there was also a big *if* in the lecture hall, *if* this is appropriate and *if* this is ultimately useful to the client, and *if* we ourselves want to do this, even where there is psychotherapeutic permission to do so. All the same, the body psychotherapists, mostly given a voice through Roz Carroll, were happy to be given long awaited recognition and felt that the split as well as the hierarchy of psychoanalysis over body psychotherapists, the mind over the body, had begun to be addressed.

Sarah Jack is a registered member of CAPP.

Bowlby Memorial Conference 2003— reading list

Aron, L., & Anderson, F. S. (Eds.) (1998). *Relational Perspectives on the Body*. Hillside, NJ: Analytic Press.

Burka, J. B. (1996). The therapist's body in reality and fantasy: A perspective from an overweight therapist. In: B. Gerson, (Ed.), *The Therapist as a Person* (pp. 255–275). Hillside NJ: Analytic Press.

Butler, J. (1993). *Bodies that Matter: On The Discursive Limits of Sex*. London: Taylor and Francis

Butler, J. (1990). *Gender Trouble: Feminism and the Subversion of Identity*. New York: Routledge.

Casement, P. (1985). *On Learning from the Patient*. London: Tavistock.

Casement, P. (2002). *Learning from our Mistakes*. Hove, East Sussex: Brunner-Routledge.

Cassidy, J., & Shaver, P. (Eds.) (1999). *Handbook of Attachment: Theory, Research, and Clinical Implications*. New York: Guilford Press.

Davies, J. M., & Frawley, G. (1994). *Treating the Adult Survivors of Childhood Sexual Abuse: A Psychoanalytic Perspective*. New York: Basic Books.

Etherington, K. (2003). *Trauma, The Body and Transformation*. London: Jessica Kingsley.

Feinberg, L. (1993). *Stone Butch Blues: A Novel*. Ithaca, NY: Firebrand Books.

Halberstam, J. (1998). *Female Masculinity*. Durham, NC: Duke University Press.

La Barre, F. (2001). *On Moving and Being Moved: Non-verbal Behaviour in Clinical Practice*. Hillside, NJ: Analytic Press.

Maroda, K. (1999). *Seduction Surrender, and Transformation; Emotional Engagement in the Analytic Process*. Hillside, NJ: Analytic Press.

McDougall, J. (1989). *Theatres of the Body: A Psychoanalytic Approach to Psychosomatic Illness*. London: Free Association Books.

Mitchell, S. A. (1988). *Relational Concepts in Psychoanalysis: An Integration*. Cambridge, MA: Harvard University Press.

Mitchell, S. A., & Aron, L. (1999). *Relational Psychoanalysis: The Emergence of a Tradition*. Hillside, NJ: Analytic Press.

Orbach, S. (1994) Working with the false body. In: A. Erskine & D. Judd (Eds.), *The Imaginative Body* (pp. 166–179). London: Whurr.

Orbach, S. (1999). *The Impossibility of Sex*. Harmondsworth: Penguin Books.

Orbach, S. (2000). False self and false body. In: B. Kahr, (Ed.), *The Legacy of Winnicott* (pp. 124–134). London: Karnac.

Orbach, S. (2001). *Hunger Strike, Starving Amidst Plenty*. London: The Other Press.

Pally, R. (2000). *The Mind–Brain Relationship*. London: Karnac.

Schwartz, J. (2000). Review Essay—A beginners guide to the brain: Ten lectures on the neurology of mental life by Mark Solms at the Anna Freud Centre. *British Journal of Psychotherapy*, 17: 173–179.

Skolnick, N. J., & Warshaw, S. C. (1992). *Relational Perspectives in Psychoanalysis*. Hillside, NJ: Analytic Press.

Stolorow, R.D., & Atwood, G.E. (1991). *The Intersubjective Foundations of Psychological Life*. Hillside, NJ: Analytic Press.

Trevarthen, C. (1998a). The concept and foundations of infant intersubjectivity. In S. Bråten (Ed.), *Intersubjective Communication and Emotion in Early Ontogeny* (pp. 15–46). Cambridge: Cambridge University Press.

Trevarthen, C., Aitken, K. J., Papoudi, D., & Robarts, J. Z. (1998). *Children with Autism: Diagnosis and Interventions to Meet their Needs* (2nd edn). London: Jessica Kingsley.

Winnicott, D. W. (1949). Mind in relation to psyche soma. *Through Paediatrics to Psychoanalysis* (pp. 243–254). London: Tavistock.

Other Resources

www.thinkbody.co.uk

Introduction to The Centre for Attachment-based Psychoanalytic Psychotherapy

The Centre for Attachment-based Psychoanalytic Psychotherapy (CAPP) is an organization committed to the development of this particular approach to psychotherapy. It provides a four-year training for psychotherapists and a consultation and referral service.

Attachment-based psychoanalytic psychotherapy has developed on the basis of the growing understanding of the importance of attachment relationships to human growth and development throughout life. This approach to psychotherapy, developing from the relational tradition of psychoanalysis, draws upon psychoanalytic insights and the rapidly growing field of attachment theory.

Understanding psychotherapy within the context of attachment relationships leads to an approach to psychotherapy as a cooperative venture between therapist and client. The aim is to develop a sufficiently secure base to enable the exploration of loss and trauma in the course of development. The therapy is designed to create a safe space in which the client can reflect upon their lived experience, their experience of relationships in the present, and their experience of their relationship with the therapist.

Mourning is vital to the acknowledgement and understanding of the effects of abandonment, loss, abuse, whether emotional, sexual, or physical. The support of an authentic process of mourning forms a central part of the therapeutic work. This is crucial to the development of a sense of self, and the capacity to form and sustain intimate relationships. Both a strong sense of self and good attachment relationships are essential to managing stressful experiences.

The losses and traumas to be addressed in therapy are not confined to a private world or to early life. Groups and society as a whole shape attachment relationships formed by individuals. The experience of loss and abuse as a result of structures and pressures and every day experiences concerning race, gender, sexuality, class, culture, and disability, together with the complexity of the individual's response, can be worked with in a profound way through attachment-based psychoanalytic psychotherapy.

John Bowlby's original development of attachment theory was promoted primarily by his concern to ensure social recognition for the central importance of attachment and the experience of loss in early development. He was also concerned to strengthen the scientific foundations for psychoanalysis. Since his original work, attachment theory has come to occupy a key position in this fast growing scientific field. Attachment theory provides a crucial link between psychoanalysis, developmental psychology, neurobiology, and the behavioural sciences.

CAPP has drawn on a wide range of approaches, including the British object relations school, the American interpersonalist school, theories on the development of the self, and contemporary work on trauma and dissociation to provide a breadth and depth of insight into the structure and dynamics of the internal world. The common themes that run through them are the importance of unconscious communication, of the transference and the counter-transference, of containment and the acceptance of difference, and an emphasis on two-person psychology.

The development of our theoretical base is a dynamic and continuing process. The Centre will continue to adapt and develop in the light of new research, contemporary developments and clinical experience.

Trustees of CAPP